Fernando Valenti

A PERFORMER'S GUIDE
TO THE
KEYBOARD PARTITAS
OF

J. S. BACH

Yale University Press
New Haven and London

Published with the assistance of the F. B. Adams, Jr.,
Publication Fund.

Many musical examples in this book are reproduced from
Johann Sebastian Bach, *Six Partitas,* edited by Richard
Douglas Jones, with the kind permission of the publisher,
Bärenreiter-Verlag, Kassel.

Designed by Nancy Ovedovitz and set in Fournier type by
G&S Typesetters, Inc. Printed in the United States of
America by Hamilton Printing Company,
Castleton, New York.

Library of Congress Cataloging-in-Publication Data
Valenti, Fernando.
A performer's guide to the keyboard partitas of J. S. Bach /
Fernando Valenti.
p.   cm.   Bibliography: p.   Includes index.
ISBN 0–300–04313–9 (alk. paper)
1. Bach, Johann Sebastian, 1685–1750.   Partitas, harpsichord, BWV
825–830.   2. Suite (Music)   3. Suites (Harpsichord)—
Analysis, appreciation.   I. Title.
ML410.B13V34   1989
786.4'0421—dc19   89–30930   CIP   MN

The paper in this book meets the guidelines for permanence
and durability of the Committee on Production Guidelines
for Book Longevity of the Council on Library Resources.

10   9   8   7   6   5   4   3   2   1

To F. Miguel Valenti
and Richard Torrence

CONTENTS

CONTENTS

INTRODUCTION

The six Partitas of Johann Sebastian Bach have remained prominent in the mainstream of keyboard performance since their first collective appearance in 1731. Together with a few other perennials, such as the *Italian* Concerto and the *Chromatic Fantasia,* they have held the onslaughts of history at bay. In doing so the Partitas have survived generations of stylistic upheaval, changes of instrument such as that from harpsichord to piano, and the questionable ministrations of performers, transcribers, and editors too often oriented to the tastes of a later age. This is particularly true of Partitas I, II, and VI, which have unaccountably been preferred as curtain-raising vehicles for recitals. But the durability of the Partitas is not their only source of interest. In addition to their intrinsic value as music, several historical facts commend them to the attention of both performers and scholars.

Origins

It is generally conceded that the six Partitas constitute Bach's first published work. A widespread but somewhat debatable conjecture has it that they were written at the rate of one partita per year, starting in 1725. However that may be, they were gathered together for publication in 1731. The words *In Verlegung des Autoris* (published by the author) and the designation "Opus 1" appear on the title page.

Together these six works formed part 1 of what would eventually become the gigantic *Clavier-Übung,* which contained four sections:

Part 1 (1731):
Six Partitas
Part 2 (1735):
Concerto in the Italian Taste
Overture in the French Manner
Part 3 (1739):
Assorted Organ Works and Four Duets
Part 4 (1742):
Aria with Thirty Variations (*Goldberg* Variations)

In 1731 Bach was about forty-six years of age and at the height of his powers. Whether or not these six suites were composed at the rate of one per year, it seems certain that Bach was able to exercise considerable control over their final appearance, a fact that endows them with indisputable authority. Moreover, since these works exist in versions written before 1731, the nature and extent of Bach's revisions can provide insights and help resolve dilemmas that often puzzle modern players. Most readily available in these earlier versions are Partitas III and VI, which appear in Anna Magdalena Bach's *Notebook* of 1725.

Partita I also appears to have an independent history easily traceable today. It was composed as a birthday gift for Emanuel Ludwig, prince of Anhalt-Cöthen, who was born on September 12, 1726. Although it is a great performance favorite today, it is doubtful that the music drew much attention at its first appearance, for Emanuel Ludwig died in the second year of his life, and the death of his father, Leopold, followed shortly thereafter. The Partita in B-flat was hardly to see the light again until 1731, when it joined the other five such works in the first installment of the *Clavier-Übung*.

Partita and Clavier-Übung

The title *Clavier-Übung* is thought to derive from the works of Johann Kuhnau, Bach's immediate predecessor at the Church of St. Thomas in Leipzig. For that matter, so does the term *partita,* when used to identify a succession of dance movements. Before Kuhnau, *partita* was likely to mean a string of variations, of which those of Girolamo Frescobaldi are among the most familiar today. In 1689 and again in 1695, Kuhnau produced compilations of suites collectively entitled *Clavier-Übung* and called each individual suite a partita. That Bach adopted this terminology is only one of many testimonies to his admiration for his older colleague. It is well known that Bach had held Kuhnau in high esteem long before there had been any question of following him at Leipzig.

The six Partitas represent Bach's very last words in the language of the suite. Accordingly, some scholars contend that they embody the composer's final attempt to emancipate the suite from strictures and stereotypes without inflicting undue violence on traditions inherited from such spiritual ancestors as Buxtehude, Froberger, and Kuhnau. For these reasons alone the Partitas radiate exceptional historical resonance and high pedagogical potency.

In spite of the historical significance of the Partitas, the reader may ask whether it is really useful to dwell at length on so small a segment of the composer's immense oeuvre. Far from being a disqualifying factor, their compactness intensifies the focus of our attention. Moreover, as will become evident in the following pages, the Partitas can serve as a key to many aspects of Bach performance. They may, indeed, be more useful for this purpose than almost any other single group of Bach's works.

The present book is the outgrowth of some thirty-five years of performing and teaching the Partitas. It is written in the conviction that any such endeavor can best be described as an illumination of the obvious—that is, of the ingredients that are intrinsic to the music. The reader is advised that the ultimately unresolvable question of instrumental specification (harpsichord, clavichord, or piano) is not dealt with; nor are a range of musicological issues which, however fascinating in themselves, are peripheral to the performer's primary concerns.

The format of the following discussions has been adopted in the interest of answering those questions that have most often been asked in the author's teaching experience. He recalls gratefully that it was the very asking of these questions that prompted whatever study and research may have borne fruit in the answers presented here. He further wishes to thank the students, colleagues, and friends who encouraged him in completing this book.

PARTITA I

Praeludium

QUESTION 1: Each of the introductory movements of the six Partitas bears a different title. This fact draws attention because it is not true of Bach's other suite collections. In comparison with some of these titles, such as the Sinfonia that opens Partita II or the Ouverture in Partita IV, the title Praeludium seems to fall rather flat. One feels almost disappointed that Bach did not exercise a little more imagination in providing a title for the very first movement of such a large aggregation of works.

ANSWER 1: Do not underestimate the title "praeludium" in any of its forms or translations wherever you may encounter it. Consider it guilty until proven innocent: it is universally recognized as an awesome historical trouble-maker. Imagine that you were to undertake a study of that word's applications throughout musical history. Even omitting early occurrences in the Roman liturgy, beginning your quest with the early lutenists, and bringing your survey down to the works of Chopin and Debussy, you would have embarked on a research project that might well transcend a lifetime. In the works of Bach alone the title is elusive. The comforting belief that a prelude is something that comes before something else can suddenly prove an untenable presumption. Some of Bach's preludes, in fact, precede nothing whatsoever—except, perhaps, another quite unrelated prelude in a different key (for example, BWV 933–938). Accordingly, think of a prelude, or a movement under the often-used Latinized title "praeludium," as one you will come to know only after much closer acquaintance. The title is deliberately nondescript and, unlike the "sinfonia" or "ouverture" you mentioned, will tell you little of what is in store.

QUESTION 2: May we start with the trill that recurs throughout the movement? This partita seems to be a favorite with both pianists and harpsichordists, but no two of either species seem to manage the trill the same way. In some cases it changes even from measure to measure and from right hand to left. I find this disconcerting.

ANSWER 2: Then you have evidently noticed that the trill is a constant factor, a character in the musical drama who shouldn't change costumes in the middle of a scene. This is no place to impose artificial variety merely to avoid an imagined monotony. Here repetition produces a cumulative effect and enables the trill to serve as a unifying element for the entire movement. (In time, moreover, you will discover that the line between "variety" and disorder is a thin one in *all* the arts.) The fact that the trill is embedded in the principal subject of the movement (ex. 1.1) makes it less eligible for interpretive meddling than if it were in a less conspicuous position.

Example 1.1. Praeludium, bar 1, right hand

Because the trill appears repeatedly in imitative and sequential passages, any change tends to disrupt its musico-rhetorical logic. Particularly on the harpsichord the trill commands immediate attention as a distinctive "sound effect." As such it should not be subjected to any modifications other than those the composer himself provides as he moves it about or changes its harmonic context. In no case, it should be noted, is such a change rhythmic or metrical.

QUESTION 3: I know from painful experience that there can be technical reasons for playing the trills unevenly. In some positions they can be so hard to execute that one alters them not intentionally but in self-defense. What then?

ANSWER 3: You are right that no theories can solve the purely technical problems of executing ornaments. On the gymnastics of trill playing I can offer only a few suggestions:

1. Be sure not to impede the movement of your fingers by eccentric postures.

2. Note that if the finger movement is normal, the problems arise not in individual fingers but in transitions between them.

3. Be careful that having to move your fingers so rapidly does not throw you into some sort of kinetic spasm. Sheer strength will not solve problems that call for lightness and speed. If you are markedly increasing the force of your finger attack on the trill, try at once to abandon this pneumatic drill approach and strive for some parity of force between the playing of the trill and that of its surrounding notes. You will need the utmost concentration both to diagnose and to solve this problem. Moreover, you can expect only limited help from your teacher, because the solution depends on your own physical sensations.

4. Preparation for a trill requires command of several notes before it, and a graceful exit demands knowledge of what is to follow. Whatever raptures may overtake you after executing a successful ornament, playing trills is a little like ringing doorbells: the act implies consequences unlikely to be long postponed.

5. Try to ensure a very firm attack—though more in the mind than with the finger—on the note immediately *before* the trill. Because all musical performance involves alternations of tension and relaxation, consciously applying tension to this note is likely to reduce inhibiting excesses of pressure on the trill itself.

6. Keep in mind that trills need not always be performed with contiguous fingers. Many players can trill reliably on fingers 2-4 or thumb-3. Even 3-5 can be used successfully. Wielding nonadjacent fingers may, however, invite a slight rotating motion of the hand. The harpsichordist in particular must be very careful of this. Unnecessary waverings of hand position can lead him to technical inaccuracies that he could have prevented.

7. Changing fingers within trills can provide excellent practice both in performance and as a technical exercise to combat eccentric hand position. For example, you might finger a right-hand trill 3–2–4–2–3–2 or 4–3–4–2–4–3, and so on.

QUESTION 4: It is obvious that the notes just before a trill can affect it, but I do not see why one should worry about the notes that follow it. After I have played a trill I feel glad just to be done with it.

ANSWER 4: That is because many modern players have come to regard trills as natural enemies. In fact, performance problems in this Praeludium have less to do with the trills than with the two or three notes that follow. Consider the following:

1. We know that Bach often wrote trill terminations either in small notes or, even more frequently, in large notes of full value.

2. We also know that terminations may often be added even when he did not bother to notate them. (For the moment, confine that particular license solely to the music of Bach. Extending it to the works of other composers is likely to be rash until we have dealt with the subject in more detail.)

3. It is accepted that the written note values of these terminations do not determine the exact speed of the trill's oscillations, nor should these note values always be taken literally for the terminations themselves. A trill-plus-termination notated thus, for instance,

would not necessarily indicate that the trill must be played in sixteenth notes corresponding to the written value of its termination, or even that the termination itself should necessarily be so played. Note well that the trill has been imposed upon a *dotted* quarter note. In some traditions a dotted note can and often should be lengthened beyond its written value. Its termination will thus be shortened.

4. Having said this, I must quickly add that this tradition of double-dotting (which will be dealt with in another context) is totally irrelevant to this Praeludium. The tyranny of the repetitive notation precludes any suggestion of rhythmic flexibility. The presence of a trill or any other ornament in the clearly assertive rhythmic figure ⁊ ♫♫ ♫♫ must not alter a single one of its more than a dozen and a half appearances.

5. From all this we may conclude that the two notes following the trill should not be taken as mere trill terminations, and that all occurrences must be kept identical so as not to undermine the nuclear rhythmic pattern.

6. Finally, a good deal of the hardship keyboard players encounter in these trills is self-imposed because they view the Praeludium as a scherzo-like piece to be essayed, in spite of internal warnings, at a dizzying speed. If a steady pulse is maintained and the requirements of the recurrent ornament fulfilled, it is nearly impossible to play or even to hear this movement at a speed much beyond that of a march. The rewards of caution are reciprocal: bringing absolute clarity to the ornaments restrains the speed, which in turn makes the trills easier to manage technically and far more impressive to hear.

QUESTION 5: If I may change the subject, here and there I find it hard to distinguish two voices. For example, in measures 6 to 8 in the right hand and 14 to 16 in the left I hear little more than chord outlines, though the stemming of the notes clearly points to polyphony.

A N S W E R 5: Your problem lies in the very simplicity of the harmony. The two voices form elementary triadic combinations that suggest leisurely broken chords rather than a two-voice texture. Let me suggest an easy rule to help out in this instance and others like it: A note following a silence or another note longer than itself must be pronounced in such a way as to make the ear aware of the reinitiation of motion in the first case, or an increase in the rate of that motion in the second. This may be achieved by touch or some other instrumental resource. In this way the listener's attention is subtly drawn to the change. On instruments such as the clavichord or the piano, which can vary the volume of tone, rigorous control must be exercised to avoid exaggerating the very slight overpronunciation. Often one need only think of the long note as a "vowel" and the following short note as a strong "consonant," such as *t, k,* or *p.* As an example, in the left hand at bar 14 (ex. 1.2), try to apply a slightly stronger finger attack on the encircled notes. Be sure, however, that you resist any temptation to overemphasize with a convulsive lurch of the hand, and that you scrupulously observe the written values of notes and rests. Thus you should find that you have (a) created an enchainment of minute but clearly audible upbeats alternating between tenor and bass lines, enhancing the impression that they are independent; and (b) lent both voices a more forward, horizontal propulsion, despite the somewhat sedentary nature of the harmony.

Example 1.2. Praeludium, bar 14

Q U E S T I O N 6: From the second half of bar 19 to the final chord of the Praeludium Bach thickens the chords to achieve a striking textural density. For example, he writes left-hand octaves for the last three eighth-note beats of bar 20 and the final chord. I have heard it argued that Bach would hardly have notated octaves for the harpsichord, since it can produce them through registration, and that this suggests that the work was intended for the clavichord, which has no such mechanical resource. What is your opinion?

ANSWER 6: The broadening of sound here is an example of "organic dynamics." It is especially effective when contrasted with the sparse texture in the following Allemande. The comments on the octaves, however, are nonsense. Octaves are common occurrences in music of this period and earlier, from the simplest continuo realization to the most technically extravagant sonatas of Domenico Scarlatti. One might perform this movement with great success on a clavichord, but to conclude from the mere presence of octaves that this was Bach's means of instrumental specification only serves to confirm that a little knowledge is a dangerous thing.

Allemande

QUESTION 1: Can you explain why this Allemande "feels" faster than the Corrente that follows it?

ANSWER 1: The texture at the start of the Allemande is thin, so the ear will perceive little more than a single line, in contrast to the massive chordal ending of the Praeludium. The long strand of sixteenth notes in the first six bars also seems to allow for greater momentum than do the more controlled and punctuated triplet figurations of the Corrente. Bars 1 to 6 of the Allemande contain little of either melodic or harmonic interest to detain the ear. "Why, then," you may ask, "should I not play fast?" Whereupon, disregarding the title, you push the pulse out of character for an allemande and into an improper relationship with the Corrente.

It will help if you take a deep breath at the end of the Praeludium and do not base the speed of the Allemande on its first six measures. Instead, choose a pulse appropriate to some musical or technical situation that comes later in the piece. This assumes that you have *studied* the Allemande before beginning to *practice* it. As many good teachers have said, before one can really "learn" these works, one must already know them. Turning a page and plunging into the music is no more than a first reading. Thoughtful preparation often requires you to revise such readings drastically and many times.

QUESTION 2: As you have said, the "long strand of sixteenth notes" at the beginning offers almost no clues to how one might shape them musically. Their appearance suggests that they should be played with absolute evenness, but I find this nearly impossible to do. In spite of my diligence, irregularities keep cropping up in my timing, attack, and release.

A N S W E R 2: You have evoked a paradox. The "evenness" you aspire to is not achieved by playing evenly; it is an illusion conjured up by a calculated *unevenness* in phrasing and articulation. In short, however much mechanical evenness you can manage, the real solutions are musical, not technical.

Q U E S T I O N 3: Would you care to recommend the proper phrasing and articulation for this particular piece?

A N S W E R 3: No. I would rather have you develop your own detective-like approach to exploring and choosing among the possibilities for performance. It is better for a teacher to help students perfect their analytical techniques and develop their reasoning processes than to dictate any formulae that are not patently incontrovertible. In this case, however, I will offer a few suggestions, if you will keep in mind that there may well be excellent alternatives.

Examine measure 1 as it appears in the 1731 version of the partita (ex. 1.3). At first glance you will assume—correctly, as far as it goes—that Bach's irregular stemming and beaming of the notes merely indicates their distribution between hands. But this alone can hardly account for the eccentric groupings: sixteen equal notes in 4/4 time beamed into five groups, two of four notes each, a third of two, and the last two of three notes each. (The earlier editors of the Bachgesellschaft retained this beaming except to give note 13 a beam of its own and a downward stem.)

Example 1.3. Allemande, bar 1, right hand

Note that one element in the notation does not change: in the openings of both sections of the Allemande, the last three notes in each measure are beamed together. Since these notes are always for the right hand, that may seem a sufficient explanation. But can we, exercising a little imagination, discover other reasons that might help reduce the exasperations caused by the "long strand of sixteenth notes"? Perhaps so.

In each of the measures under discussion the fourth note from the end could easily be played by the right hand as well. May there not then be some other reason for grouping only the last three together? The first two of these notes in bar 1 form an augmented fourth that implies a seventh chord. After the unbroken adherence to the B-flat triad in the previous thirteen notes, this is an important harmonic event. Might we not enhance this function by over-holding these notes slightly, almost as if they had been written thus:

The last three notes catapult you across the bar line, because the harmonic tension they have introduced must be resolved. You might therefore decide to subject the A-flat to a slightly stronger attack. This slight deviation of touch would emphasize the harmonic function of the three notes by overlapping them into a chord and drawing attention to the resolution-demanding dissonance.

This sort of reading between the lines may often solve problems that mere mechanics cannot. It may also suggest that the perfect evenness you sought was hard to achieve less because it was technically difficult than because it was just plain wrong. These techniques of minute dissection may seem to belong less to music than to microsurgery, but they will eventually become intuitive second nature, rather like choosing the right word in a language you speak fluently.

QUESTION 4: While the microscope is handy, will you tell me whether the ornament symbols at bars 12, 14, and 15 (ex. 1.4) really represent trills?

Example 1.4. Allemande, bars 12–15

ANSWER 4: Unless the pulse you adopt is inordinately rapid, I do not see why you should doubt it. If, however, you are really asking, "Need I start the trills from the note above even though it has just been sounded?" I will surprise you by offering the conventional textbook answer: Yes. (This subject is discussed in more detail in connection with the Sinfonia of Partita II.) In doing so you will be supported by the most celebrated ornament tables and treatises. Besides, it is too early for you to open Pandora's box. The lid is already a bit wobbly.

Corrente

QUESTION 1: Given the triplet motion that pervades this movement, where does one place the left-hand sixteenth note in figures like the one in bars 1 and 2 (ex. 1.5)?

Example 1.5. Corrente, bars 1–2

ANSWER 1: It should be aligned with the third note of the triplet. You may find this contradicted by Johann Joachim Quantz (*Versuch einer Anweisung die Flöte traversiere zu spielen*, 1752) but amply supported by a majority of contemporary authorities east and west of the Rhine, including C. P. E. Bach (*Versuch über die wahre Art das Clavier zu spielen*, 1753 and 1762). Quantz's view still has a number of devoted and vociferous adherents, but it can lead to occasional shipwrecks in performance. We will have more to say about "assimilation" into triplet motion when we come to the Allemande of Partita V.

QUESTION 2: Where would you suggest one search for clues to determine the proper tempo for this piece?

ANSWER 2: There are a number of speed controls that will not inhibit the natural tendency of correntes to be rather fast. Notice that melodic statements and harmonic events are seldom confined within the bounds of any single triplet. Since no triplet is totally independent of its predecessor or successor, you cannot "ride" them into the realm of the hysterical. Moreover, many of the triplets initiate motion on their second note, the first being tied

over from a previous event. In such cases you are helpless to activate the triplet from its first note, a practice that offers an often irresistible temptation to
stamp on inanimate downbeats and gain speed. Instead, you must use the second or third note of the triplets, or occasionally both. Thus, technical kinetics,
as well as the melodic and harmonic character of the music, demand that the
Corrente not be played excessively fast. Add to this the punctuating effect of
the concurrent dotted motion and I do not foresee too many sins of speed. It
goes without saying that you must also have very firmly in mind what you
have just finished doing in the Allemande. In most suites, the relationship between these two types of movements is especially close.

Sarabande

QUESTION 1: At first glance this Sarabande appears rather wayward
and disjointed, almost like a recitative. This sort of thing can go a long way
toward unnerving a keyboard player, since many of his favorite resources
seem out of reach. Among these are a clear and steady pulse based on the
music's original choreographic requirements and the fundamental ingredient
of melodic continuity.

ANSWER 1: I remember your outcry about the allegedly unmanageable
symmetry of long strings of sixteenth notes in the Allemande. Now you seem
to be complaining about exactly the opposite. Too much freedom, you claim,
and too many irregularities for the player to impose any order. Let me say
that your words "appears rather wayward" suggest that you have not actually
heard this Sarabande but are judging it from the note-picture on the page. No
harm done; you have to start somewhere. Now let us build on these beginnings, certain that you will soon begin to experience this movement in actual
sound. In your search for order, measures 9 and 10 (ex. 1.6) will be a good
place to start.

Example 1.6. Sarabande, bars 9–10, right hand

Observe that each bar contains a sequence, a musical gesture exactly repeated
at different pitch levels. This is musical order and symmetry with a will. Next
notice the frequent intensification of gravity imposed on the second beats of

measures, a common characteristic of sarabandes. In bar 1 (ex. 1.7) this is achieved by the appearance of an octave in the left hand.

Example 1.7. Sarabande, bar 1

In measures 5 and 6, this intensification is achieved even more effectively by amassing harmonic tension and textural density (ex. 1.8).

Example 1.8. Sarabande, bars 5–6

In your search for clues, you will also count twelve out of twenty-eight measures in which no activity at all takes place on left-hand third beats. This is worth mentioning not only because the ear often perceives the silent third beats as a retroactive strengthening of second beats, but also because whatever "waywardness" you perceive in this movement most conspicuously appears on these bassless third beats. This means that you are not likely to go too far astray on improvisatory third beats, because the bar line will appear soon enough to control you. Here, then, is another force for order.

QUESTION 2: Now please say what you can to identify the ornament in the right hand of bar 21 (ex. 1.9). Since the symbol clearly implies some sort of trill, how long do you think it should last? It seems impossible that Bach could want it rattling away until the first sixteenth note of measure 23.

Example 1.9. Sarabande, bars 21–23

ANSWER 2: According to Bach's own table of ornaments in the *Clavier-Büchlein* (an instruction book intended for his eldest son, Wilhelm Friedemann), this ornament is a *Doppelt-Cadence,* and it denotes

Parenthetically, notice the clash created by an identical ornament at bar 26 (ex. 1.10), where it forces a false relation between the ornament's own D-natural and the D-flat in the right hand.

Example 1.10. Sarabande, bar 26

As for the duration of the trill, some would say that, strictly speaking, it should continue through the written length of the note. Because of the ties, this would carry you to the first sixteenth note of bar 23—but that must depend somewhat on how "strictly" you want to speak. There would seem little question that the purpose of the ornament is to prolong the sound so that the right-hand E-flat can operate as a type of inverted pedal-point. Nevertheless, a cessation of the trill (or *point d'arrêt,* as the French call it) may be determined, preferably somewhere well before the first beat of bar 23, and perhaps as early as the last four left-hand sixteenth notes in bar 22. This would not require releasing the E-flat itself, but merely stopping the trill oscillations. Whatever reprisals the latter suggestion may evoke from the more literal-minded, it stands to reason that a sensible player will want to relieve the listener's ear in ample time for it to hear clearly the resumption of motion in the right hand, starting on the second note of bar 23.

The left-hand situation in bar 26 is somewhat different, since Bach actually provides a termination for the trill. Here the choices seem somewhat better defined. If you stop the trill too long before the termination, you will dissociate the one from the other. With a few debatable exceptions, this is strikingly unstylish in Bach. (You may wish to look at a few moments in the "Overture in the French Manner" from the *Clavier-Übung,* part 2, for what seem to be exceptions to the practice of merging trills into their notated endings.) If you attempt to render the present termination longer, by expanding it to sixteenth notes, for example, you will create parallel fifths with the right hand. You would then seem to have two legitimate choices: to play the termination exactly as written, or to play it *after* the right hand has struck its final note. Although the latter is my preference, it would hardly reduce the length of the trill, which seems to be the outcome you desired.

The best advice may still be to take the fullest advantage of the prefix to the trill at bar 21, to start the trill itself at less than full speed, and then to increase that speed by "imperceptible gradations," as Couperin wrote,* never forgetting to predetermine a point d'arrêt that collaborates well with the activity of the left hand and does not leave the ear in a musical lurch.

Q U E S T I O N 3: Do I see an allusion to the principal motif of the Praeludium at bar 19 of this Sarabande (ex. 1.11)?

Example 1.11. Sarabande, bar 19

A N S W E R 3: I see no great harm in regarding it as such if you wish. It is fairly pointless, however. The bon-bon of thematic interrelationships between movements of the Partitas has been chewed and eschewed by many of our most expert bon-bon purveyors over the last century or so. To extend your idea to the edge of absurdity, skip forward to the Sarabande of Partita VI. There, at bars 13 and 14, you will find the same musical pattern. Will this also induce you to infer thematic interrelation with the Praeludium of Partita I?

Q U E S T I O N 4: Am I correct in assuming that a discreet chord rolling is permissible in thick textures? The thought comes to mind in slow movements such as this, where chords sound flat and two-dimensional on the harpsichord if they are laid down precisely.

A N S W E R 4: On plucked string instruments you must effect these slight strummings with care. You will want them to sound free and spontaneous, but paradoxically this can only be achieved through rigorous premeditation.

*In "Le rossignol en amour," *Oeuvres complètes,* ed. Maurice Canchie, vol. 4 (Paris, 1932), 31.

Some advice is in order here:

1. It is doubtful that the same degree of arpeggiation will prove successful if heard repeatedly.

2. You must assure yourself that the chord in question contains a sufficient number of notes. One would not, for example, make a practice of rolling thirds or octaves, or for that matter any vertical combination of fewer than three notes, unless there are indications to do so in the notation.

3. Even greater care must be exercised in rolling chords that contain significant dissonances. The strumming must not be allowed to reduce the friction between the dissonant notes and the main harmonic fibre. Some of Domenico Scarlatti's most striking effects are spoiled when treated in this fashion.

4. Be alert to signposts that steer you away from these strummings by offering other devices, such as ornamentation, to eliminate the thudding caused by an absolutely precise attack. The chord on the first beat of bar 2 (ex. 1.12) is an example: the ornament on the uppermost note may easily replace the slight arpeggiation that you might otherwise have thought necessary.

Example 1.12. Sarabande, bar 2, with upbeat

In addition to relieving heavy-footedness, these slight chord rollings can clarify the conduct of polyphonic voices and help prolong tone duration. Arpeggiations are often used, and sometimes abused, by continuo accompanists for this purpose.

QUESTION 5: In measure 20 (ex. 1.13), are the notes indicated by arrows B-flats or B-naturals?

Example 1.13. Sarabande, bar 20, right hand

ANSWER 5: Surveying all the sources presently available (see list of sources and editions at end of book), you will find that a natural sign appears only in the one housed in the Staatsbibliothek Preussischer Kulturbesitz in West Berlin. Contemporary editors are understandably put out by this lack of consensus and resort to some truly extraordinary footnoting to justify retaining the B-flat against all musical logic. One otherwise almost unimpeachable edition, Henle 1952, even cites a "modulation" to B-flat major. This is preposterous. There is no such modulation and Bach has devoted considerable attention in measure 19 to establishing the key of C minor. Consensus or not, there is no doubt that the notes should be B-naturals.

Menuets I and II

QUESTION 1: Is this a French spelling of the title?

ANSWER 1: Yes. The Italian version of the word is usually "minuetto." Later on, in Partita V, you will see "minuetta," which is wrong in any language! Like the English word *minute,* menuet connotes smallness. Needless to say, this quality is by no means always observable in Baroque minuets, and even less in those of the classical period. The minuet is only one of the various miscellaneous and optional dances—gavottes, passepieds, bourrées, and so on—that can appear in Bach's suites. In this partita, a second minuet follows the first. The traditional procedure is to play Menuet I with all repeats, then Menuet II with all repeats, and finally Menuet I again, this time with no repeats. This approximation of an A–B–A form is often alluded to in "music appreciation" classes, but you will not see it again in the six Partitas. It is not, however, uncommon in some of Bach's other suite collections. The four orchestral Suites or Overtures, the so-called English Suites, and the "French Overture" in part 2 of the *Clavier-Übung* readily come to mind.

QUESTION 2: In the Allemande we agreed that the thinness of texture might provoke excessive speed. Does Menuet I not offer a similar temptation?

ANSWER 2: Again your impression seems to be almost entirely visual. Here, as well as in many other works you will have occasion to play, it may be useful to remember that the "minuetness" resides in the quarter notes in the left hand. Anyone foolish enough to attempt these at high speed will soon see how irretrievably this alienates him from the spirit of the dance. Moreover, much of what we know about baroque performance practices suggests that such thinness does not exist here at all, except, perhaps, in the notation. In example 1.14, upward stems indicate the melodically active notes of the right hand.

Example 1.14. Menuet I, bars 1–4, rewritten to emphasize melodic line

In effect, a third voice has been added in bars 1 through 4, a procedure that would have been considered legitimate by any performer in Bach's time.

QUESTION 3: This idea is attractive, but would it not invite all manner of distortions at the hands of pianists?

ANSWER 3: Only if they viewed the upward-stemming in example 1.14 as calling for these notes to be played disproportionately louder. We all know the often unstylistic results of pianistic muscularity and the tendency of pianists to solve nondynamic problems by dynamic means. And who can blame them? They make their music, after all, on an instrument of which spontaneously imposed dynamic nuance is the basic language. It is all the more important, then, for pianists to realize that punching out the upward-stemmed notes in the above example is totally irrelevant to what is being illustrated. They may soon see that if any prominence is desirable for certain notes, it is to be achieved by tone duration, not by added loudness.

QUESTION 4: If Bach wanted the passage to be played this way, why did he not write it so? It would seem to have been well within the compass of his habits of notation.

ANSWER 4: There are a number of answers, of which two most readily come to mind. Insofar as double-stemming the notes would commit Bach to three-voice writing throughout the Menuet, he might not have wished to be held accountable for it. Both you and I can see places in this movement where we might not wish to follow the procedure shown above (in bar 7, for example). Furthermore, Bach may well have assumed that any intelligent player would think of this performance device without a written prescription. In one often-cited case he did exactly the opposite: he revised the notation of certain lengthened notes in "Les bergeries" from François Couperin's *Sixième ordre,* apparently certain that virtually any player would sustain them anyway (exx. 1.15 and 1.16).

Example 1.15. Passage from Couperin's "Bergeries"

Example 1.16. The same, as notated in Anna Magdalena Bach's *Notebook*

Q U E S T I O N   5: In Menuet II, I seem to see some sort of part-song, perhaps even a rather carelessly written chorale.

A N S W E R   5: Menuet II is, indeed, written in four voices for much of the time. Rather than deplore it as a "carelessly written chorale," however, why not try to imagine that you are reviewing it for a local music journal in 1731? You might write something like this:

"In contrast to Menuet I, Menuet II is texturally heavy, its sound therefore less ductile, and its motion rather more stolid. These characteristics enhance the contrast undoubtedly intended between the two minuets. Its bass line tends to be sustained, rather than rhythmically active. This produces a droning quality, vaguely reminiscent of such middle sections as the second Gavotte of the G minor English Suite, one of Bach's unsurpassable 'drone' movements. This leaning toward comparatively inanimate bass lines and occasional thickness of texture is by no means an uncommon feature of these tripartite formulations."

Were you to write such a review, you would, without presuming to deliver any staggering revelations, establish that you knew how Menuet II should sound.

Q U E S T I O N   6: Given the desire to contrast the two Menuets, is it absolutely necessary to maintain the same performance pulse for both?

ANSWER 6: You will have to make up your own mind. Eighteenth-century authorities are ominously quiet on this subject. It may be useful to remember, however, that Bach's dance movements are concert versions or even paraphrases of the originals that were actually danced. It would not be unreasonable to attribute to these later versions certain innate flexibilities. You may, then, consider a slight change in pulse to be an indispensable ingredient of the contrast that is called for between the two Menuets. On the other hand, you may conclude that the essence of the contrast lies elsewhere than in a change of speed and, accordingly, choose to forgo it.

QUESTION 7: What do you consider a reasonable duration for the small-note appoggiaturas at bars 8 and 15 (ex. 1.17)?

Example 1.17. Menuet II, bars 8 and 15

ANSWER 7: Although both appoggiaturas are written as eighth notes, you are to be commended for not taking their written values too literally. Their length depends on the context in which they occur. For example, you will wish to consider the general character of Menuet II. It might strike you that a short, abrupt sound jars with the piece's rather sedate musical countenance. You would then choose to play an eighth-note appoggiatura as written. You may even want to lengthen it in bar 8, since the melodic motion does not resume immediately in the same voice. Bar 15 presents different problems, because the oncoming melodic event on the third beat allows less time for a long appoggiatura. You may still retain a certain amount of initiative, however, particularly since it would be difficult to establish an inviolable melodic parallelism between the two bars. There is, therefore, very little to suggest that they must be played identically.

At bar 15 you may wish to clarify the $^6_4$–to–$^5_3$ harmonic relationship that would result on the first two beats. In that case you would lengthen the appoggiatura to a quarter note. You might then ask why Bach wrote a small note at all, since a quarter note would be a full-fledged member of a simple harmony (a $^6_4$ chord on the first beat) and deprive it of the ornamental qualifications that would have justified the small print. On the other hand, you may be taken with the not unattractive idea of a shorter appoggiatura in order to clear the air for the motion of the tenor voice on the second and third beats of bar 15. Musical thinking must go beyond mere mechanical considerations to determine the *purpose* of the ornamental note and how this can best be made clear to the listener.

Giga

QUESTION 1: Whence comes the Italian title, rather than the usual French version "gigue" or its quaint corruption "gique"?

ANSWER 1: This form of the title is found in the 1731 sources, but you are quite right to be surprised. Even editions that claim to reproduce original texts scrupulously have unaccountably substituted "Gigue" for the Italian title.

QUESTION 2: Dare I venture the guess that Bach's use of the Italian word supports the oft-murmured suspicion that he learned all there was to learn about hand-crossings (which are outlandishly in evidence in this Giga) from Domenico Scarlatti, who enjoyed virtually exclusive ownership of them? Or that an Italian title is appropriate because Scarlatti was Italian by birth? I believe Philipp Spitta makes some comment to that effect.

ANSWER 2: Rubbish! There is no evidence that Bach had any direct contact whatsoever with Scarlatti or his keyboard music. Furthermore, it is pathetically wrong to perpetuate the notion that Scarlatti was the only or even the first composer to use hand-crossings. He used them abundantly, purposefully, and with a skill never surpassed, but he was in no way their originator. It would also be difficult to defend the contention that hand-crossings were an exclusively Italian phenomenon. A sizable collection could be made of non-Italian music that incorporates hand-crossings. Such an anthology would include a minuet (Wotquenne 111) written by C. P. E. Bach and engraved by him in 1731, the very year in which Johann Sebastian compiled the six Partitas. In the young Bach's brief autobiography (1773), he refers to this work as "a minuet set for keyboard with hand-crossings," adding parenthetically that it was "an idiomatic and then very clever trick."*

---

*Cited in Charles Burney's *Tagebuch einer musikalischen Reise,* translated into German by C. D. Ebeling (1772–73; reprint, Kassel, 1959), 3:203.

ANSWER 2: It is important to reexamine the Italian terminology. Adagio, for example, means "leisurely" or "at your ease." This is, to say the least, imprecise as an indication of pulse and can raise many more questions than it answers. Furthermore, it is markedly controversial historically. Whereas today we think of adagio as meaning rather slow, C. P. E. Bach, Purcell, Quantz, and others warned against this interpretation. No one has actually considered adagio to mean *fast,* but the seventeenth and eighteenth centuries seem to have construed it as indicating a moderate speed. This differs somewhat from the word's connotations in the classical period, the nineteenth century, and our own day.

If you add to this that the marking *grave* describes character more than it defines speed, and is thus equally vague, the seeds of your mistrust should by now have borne fruit. Granted that fastness and slowness are themselves relative concepts—a fact that we will presently use to advantage—imposing nebulous guidelines still offers some threat to the interpreter.

The term *andante* has a similarly complicated history. Although it clearly seems to mean "at a walking speed," the ground at times stirs tremulously beneath your feet. Domenico Scarlatti, for examples, marked "allegro andante" atop his Sonata K. 343 and other works. Handel used "andante allegro" several times. Such seemingly contradictory indications, while not totally incomprehensible, are not what a modern musician has been trained to expect.

Finally, the change of signature from c to 3/4 gives virtually no inkling of speed. Before Bach's day time signatures were far more helpful, but in this case there is nothing inherent in the numbers 3/4 that can justify the Olympic velocities undertaken by many keyboard players. In short, the headings of the three sections of the Sinfonia are not the only places to seek clues to their respective speeds.

QUESTION 3: You have not answered my question. Having undermined my confidence in these as well as other Italian markings, it is only fair that you should now make some positive suggestions.

ANSWER 3: Notice that the word *tempo* was rigorously avoided in Answer 2. My remarks about indications such as grave adagio, andante, or even the change of time signature at bar 30 focused on their imprecision as determinants of *speed* or *pulse.*

If we use tempo to signify the rate of movement or animation within any given section, we can attempt an interesting experiment: Play all three sections in proper sequence at the same speed, with such uniformity as can be measured by an unchanging tapping of your foot, of someone else's foot, or, if worse comes to worst, by a metronome. You will notice that, although the speed remains unchanged, the *tempo* will vary from section to section, according to the nature and degree of activity within them. Among the results will be that:

1. You will have provided yourself with a clear illustration of the difference between tempo and mere speed.

2. The "contrast" you mentioned in your question is achieved by the differing nature of the music, regardless of the uniform metronomic speed.

3. The Italian markings now seem more welcome as confirmation of what the music is going to do in any case.

4. The constant pulse operates much as mortar serves bricks: it keeps the sections somewhat apart, while firmly holding them together in the interest of evolving a larger structure.

Q U E S T I O N 4 : A fascinating idea, but I must now undertake to guess what pulse might prove suitable for all three sections, at least in the initial stages of the experiment.

A N S W E R 4 : That ought not to be difficult. The Grave adagio will probably not help you in choosing, for its motion is largely sporadic. The Andante might do, provided you can retain the "walking" image. Perhaps the 3/4 section is the best hunting ground because, as the most active area, it will probably be the first to sound perfectly dreadful if your choice of speed should prove wrong. Let me remind you that, when we spoke of the Allemande in Partita I, you noted advantages in deriving speed from active or "difficult" sections of movements.

Q U E S T I O N 5 : Assuming that I have settled on a pulse, experimental or otherwise, is it to be suspended at measures 28 and 29 (ex. 2.1)? I have in mind a broad ritardando for the ending of the Andante, and I have never heard this work performed without one.

A N S W E R 5 : The pulse will have to flex momentarily at the fermata on the first note of bar 28; a slight but tasteful broadening can perhaps mark the resumption of motion afterwards. In cadential passages such as these (the

Example 2.1. Sinfonia, bars 28–29

Well-Tempered Clavier offers many more examples) a performer is wise to ac-
knowledge that most of the desired variation in pulse is provided for by the
notes themselves. The impression of ritardando to emphasize an ending is
generated organically.

Indeed, if you play bars 28 and 29 exactly as written, it will sound as if you
were indulging in all the necessary flourishes and improvisatory fancies appropriate to such cadential passages. It is quite understandable that many
should disagree with this rather antiseptic approach, but, for purposes of the
experiment, it is prudent to recall that you must return to the basic pulse after
the first eighth note of bar 30. Too much waywardness in bars 28 and 29
might easily disturb your focus.

QUESTION 6: In bar 5 (ex. 2.2), can any known remedy ease the awkwardness of the trill on A-flat in the bass?

Example 2.2. Sinfonia, bar 5

ANSWER 6: Nothing I know of can mitigate its clumsiness or prevent it from sounding a bit like a digestive noise in such a low range of the keyboard. Some players have felt that lingering on the first note of the trill improves both sound and execution; others have suggested that it helps to add a termination downward to the G. Pianists can often arrive at other solutions due to the blessings of St. Steinway. But the situation always requires special attention.

QUESTION 7: Can you comment further on the Grave adagio? Short as it may look on paper, it seems to stumble along as if I were a string orchestra.

ANSWER 7: There are several partial remedies to your problem:

1. Consider when, if, and how you can arpeggiate some chords. Remember the warning issued in the Sarabande of Partita I not to roll all chords the same way, without taking their circumstances or harmonic content into consideration.

2. In rolling chords, be careful not to obscure notes that conspicuously belong to a melodic progression. For example, in bar 1 (ex. 2.3) the top voice of the first chord must remain clear or the subsequent figure in the right hand will appear to have come from nowhere.

Example 2.3. Sinfonia, bar 1

Here and elsewhere you might resort to a slight strumming only in the left hand. The possibilities of arpeggiation can vary greatly in character, speed, intention, and result.

3. Throughout the Grave adagio especially, assure yourself that the silences between the various spurts of motion are perfectly measured. The rests are as important as the notes themselves. Try to think of them as a sculptor considers the light and space around the marble he is chiseling.

4. The second beat of bar 6 (ex. 2.4) demands a left-hand stretch beyond the normal octave range of the hand, with no possibility of juggling notes between hands to solve the problem. This is comparatively rare. Notice, however, that the A-flat on beat 2 is tied over and therefore has the advantage of a

previous preparation. The execution should not be nearly as difficult as it appears in print.

Example 2.4. Sinfonia, bar 6

The subject of over-dotting arises here, but will be dealt with later. Meanwhile, a final warning should be issued against permitting the sound of the instrument, particularly the harpsichord, to push your imagination into a corner. If, as you fear, you are expected to be a string orchestra, try to delude yourself that you are!

QUESTION 8: Should a harpsichordist change registration at the dividing points of this Sinfonia, given its overall length and the changes in the expressive character of the music?

ANSWER 8: Changes and choices of registration will depend in part on the characteristics of the instrument at hand. Has it one or two manuals? What is the relationship of their respective sonorities? How accessible are the registration levers? In short, what is the disposition of the harpsichord? You must judge whether musical logic—or just sufficient pauses—will permit one or more free hands to adjust the levers or change manuals. For example, bar 7, immediately preceding the Andante section, ends in a sustained chord. I see nothing to prevent the player's changing keyboards or making other changes if he wishes. But at bar 30, though it seems appropriate to introduce another tone color for the fugal section, the practical difficulties are more formidable.

Remember to ask yourself repeatedly why registration indications are almost nonexistent in harpsichord music of the eighteenth century. If you agree that one reason is simply the impracticability of the composer's predicting the nature of every instrument on which his music could be played, you are ready to consider a factor on a higher artistic level: The difference in expressive languages in the Sinfonia's three sections, which might lead you to contemplate registration changes, may be the very force that precludes their necessity.

This is analogous to retaining the same pulse for all the sections in order to leave the differences in inner motion to project themselves on their own terms. (See Answer 3 above.)

QUESTION 9: I seem to have an aversion to diminutive note values running all over the page, much as I did in the Sarabande of Partita I. I would ask you to provide some keys to this Andante.

ANSWER 9: Visual impressions provide some of life's great beauties, but you may be going too far. The black page here has nothing to do with what occurred in the Sarabande. I have two simple suggestions:

   1. As you did in the Sarabande, look for sequences that refute your impression of rambling. Measures 10 and 11 (ex. 2.5) will do well for the purpose.

Example 2.5. Sinfonia, bars 10–11

   2. The unchanging eighth-note motion in the left hand will provide your ultimate control. This is a feature that you could not rely upon in the Sarabande. Think of your left hand as a cellist playing a subsidiary but vitally important role. On his steadiness depends the *andare* of the Andante. You may even find it good practice to play the left-hand part while singing the right-hand part, or at least following it with your eyes. You will soon see that the improvisatory peregrinations of the upper part can succeed only if contrasted with nearly inexorable motion in the bass.

QUESTION 10: From your mention of a cellist I infer that you do not approve of the staccato that pianists often inflict upon left-hand accompaniments—although I cannot claim that I have ever heard such a treatment of this particular piece.

ANSWER 10: This is a crucial issue. The staccato misconception persists in a great deal of Bach piano playing. Such detachments on seeing a clearly designed continuo part in the left hand are mindless and should be ruthlessly discouraged, almost without exception. They betray a complete lack of understanding of what might be called the continuo mentality. No cellist, real or imaginary, can be asked to play spiccato throughout an entire movement—he is not paid that much! A constant staccato precludes both the necessity and the possibility of phrasing—an almost inevitable result of detachments that isolate every note from every other. Some players harbor the notion that these quaint effects provide a touch of antiquity. This nonsense also deserves to be stamped out.

QUESTION 11: Is it your opinion that the subject of the fugue creates problems by being more than three measures in length?

ANSWER 11: Not really, since its rhythmic contours are so well defined. Unless it is maltreated, the subject will make its presence known. It is true, however, that some rather long fugue subjects consisting primarily of even notes require the player to probe more deeply into their harmonic implications before they can be given shape.

Bear in mind that the present fugue, despite the astonishing richness of its effect, is made of only two voices. You will then realize that it is largely the location of the subject entrances and their proper pronunciation that often gives the impression of a more complex texture. This is one of Bach's minor miracles. You must protect these entrances with carefully planned phrasings and articulations and guarantee their absolute unanimity each time they occur.

QUESTION 12: Are measures 61 and 62 (ex. 2.6) another instance of a built-in ritard, requiring obedience rather than initiative from the performer?

Example 2.6. Sinfonia, bars 61–62

ANSWER 12: Strictly speaking, yes—but your wording dehumanizes the issue. My sole objective in proposing that you approach cadential measures literally, without tampering, was to sharpen your analytical process, not to impose a mindless military discipline. Before you undertake the most reasonable flexings of meter or pulse, is it not wise to learn all you can about the musical fibre of that from which you would depart? Consider three possibilities that are particularly evident in ritards:

1. You play more slowly simply because you are playing less fast. That is *not* the meaning of ritardando.

2. On analysis you conclude that the music slows down naturally without your participation.

3. Your analysis reveals that the nature of the writing suggests a special rhetoric in which you definitely need to participate in order to ensure, even to enhance, the desired effect, always within the bounds of its own guidelines.

Choose one of these attitudes as an important part of your own artistic endeavor. Depend, however, on the reassuring verity that knowing what you are doing does not pose a threat to your creativity and inspiration.

QUESTION 13: Do I see a tied trill on the third beat of bar 61, and if so, have you any comments on it?

ANSWER 13: The tie distinguishes this ornament from an ordinary trill, usually signaled by the symbol ⌇ or the abbreviation "tr.," which is expected to begin on the beat, as well as on the upper neighbor of the note on which the symbol is imposed. François Couperin calls the tied trill a *tremblement lié.* The Germans' endless search for linguistic euphony causes them to name it *angeschlossener* or *gebundener Triller.* Johann Sebastian Bach does not literally account for this ornament in his table for Wilhelm Friedemann but makes abundant use of it throughout his music. In the course of the six Partitas we will encounter it innumerable times. The only ornament in the Bach table that approaches the tremblement lié is the *Accent und Trillo,* which, together with Couperin's model, you can see in examples 2.7 and 2.8.

Example 2.7. *Accent und Trillo* from *Clavier-Büchlein* (1720)

Example 2.8. *Tremblement lié* from *L'art de toucher le clavecin* (1717)

32

Strictly speaking, the tied trill begins not on the main note but on its upper neighbor, as does any other eighteenth-century trill, except that this upper neighbor is already sounding through the tie.

Allemande

QUESTION 1: Something about this Allemande seems to slip through my fingers. In playing it I seem to miss the point—not to mention that I rarely play it twice the same way. Can you comment?

ANSWER 1: Your question suggests that you are aware of some incongruity between the expressive content of the piece and the harpsichord's capacity to represent it. The better part of valor would be for me to leave the matter alone and merely say that Bach often transcends his medium. As performers, however, we have a responsibility beyond that recognition. I will make two suggestions. First, notice Bach's seeming subtle allusions to music for strings. Stretch your imagination to find a resemblance between the following measures of the Sonata in G minor for unaccompanied violin (ex. 2.9) and the right-hand part of this Allemande at measures 3 and 4 (ex. 2.10).

Example 2.9. Sonata in G minor for unaccompanied violin, Presto, bars 12–14

Example 2.10. Allemande, bars 3–4, right hand

The encircled notes dip out of range momentarily—a typical and necessary means in much nonkeyboard music of confirming or altering the prevailing harmony. If this seems to you a far-fetched analogy, move forward to measures 13 and 14 in the left hand (ex. 2.11). How often have you heard similar figurations played by a cello, whether solo or in an orchestra?

Example 2.11. Allemande, bars 13–14, left hand

My second suggestion is to try dividing the long sixteenth-note line into two voices in bar 1 and equivalent situations. In measure 5 (ex. 2.12) Bach does it for you himself.

Example 2.12. Allemande, bar 5, right hand

The idea behind this exercise is not merely to divide and conquer the single line, but also to force holding over certain notes so as to push the legato and cantabile capabilities of the harpsichord to their limits. These suggestions will bring incomplete success, but there is little else to help in these situations, and you will encounter more of them as you go on.

QUESTION 2: This Allemande begins with a three-note upbeat. Is this a frequent occurrence in Bach?

ANSWER 2: Few Bach allemandes are similarly endowed. More importantly, however, these three notes initiate a sequence that you can follow for quite a while and revert to when the occasion arises. They will prevent you from contemplating ritardandi at any endings except the last. Since your speed will not be great in this movement, a little stretching and swooning at these points is not beyond temptation for any of us. Do not attempt it. If you do you will displace the upbeat and find it very difficult to restore its metrical position afterwards.

QUESTION 3: My edition has an arpeggiation sign on the second eighth-note chord at bar 32, but it omits the marking at bar 16 (ex. 2.13), a situation that is very similar, if not exactly parallel. Is this merely a slip of the pen?

ANSWER 3: Perhaps, but the discrepancy may also be attributed to the

Example 2.13. Allemande, bars 16 and 32

fact that the chord at bar 32 is composed of four notes closely spaced, whereas that at bar 16 contains only three notes somewhat farther apart. The undesirable thud of precisely simultaneous attack might have seemed to require more alleviation at bar 32. The matter is largely academic, however, since players are likely to resort to a slightly strummed delivery in both cases almost intuitively.

QUESTION 4: In the first full measure of the second half, one sometimes sees the pattern ♩♫♩ and sometimes ♩♫♩ . The discrepancy cannot help appearing to be an orthographic error, despite Hans Bischoff's claim* that it is a "rhythmic variant"—an unconvincing explanation, particularly in the light of the first right-hand beat of bar 22. Can you comment?

ANSWER 4: The ♩♫♩ is correct in bars 17 and 18, and obviously on the first beat of bar 22.

QUESTION 5: Are the right-hand trills at measures 9 and 10 (ex. 2.14) tied trills? Some printed versions show a slur from the note before the trill and some do not. Which is right?

Example 2.14. Allemande, bars 9–10

ANSWER 5: They are tied trills, including the third beat of bar 10, where

*J. S. Bach, *Six Partitas and Overture in French Style,* ed. Hans Bischoff (1882; reprint, New York, 1942), 21*n1.*

some editions omit the trill symbol itself, or present it apologetically in smaller print or in parentheses.

Courante

QUESTION 1: What are the similarities and differences between a *corrente* and a *courante*, other than the fact that the first is an Italian version of the title and the second French?

ANSWER 1: Courantes and correntes derive their titles from the verb "to run" in their respective languages. They are both intended to contrast with a preceding allemande, in the tradition of the pavane-gaillarde juxtaposition from which the allemande-courante unit is often said to derive historically. In suites that begin with a French overture, the allemande is traditionally omitted and the courante directly follows the overture. Examples of this can be seen in Bach's four orchestral Suites and in the "Overture in the French Manner" in part 2 of the *Clavier-Übung*. (We will have occasion to return to this subject in examining Partita IV.) Both courante and corrente exploit triple time, in contrast to the "square" time of whatever movement immediately precedes them. In the Bach suites both French and Italian versions are in binary form, each half being repeated, and tend to begin with an upbeat.

The disparities between courante and corrente are somewhat more difficult to define, although they are marked enough to cause you to disregard editions, the Bachgesellschaft among them, that uniformly entitle these movements "courante." In general, the courante tends to be more contrived and complex, and its motion is more varied rhythmically. (You may wish to glance ahead and compare the Corrente of Partita V, with its incessant motion in sixteenth notes, with the Courantes of either Partita II or Partita IV.) In courantes both dotted motion and suggestions of polyphonic treatment are quite common, as are alternations of 6/4 and 3/2 meters. Largely because of these internal complexities, courantes rarely invite the breezier, more headlong performance that seems appropriate to the corrente.

QUESTION 2: Even at the somewhat poised speed of a French courante, the groups of sixteenth notes scattered throughout this movement have a jarring effect on the ear. In certain positions they seem quite normal, but in others one has the feeling that they are nervous outcroppings.

ANSWER 2: The assault on the ear is intended, so as to qualify them as unifying, almost nuclear musical gestures in the movement. They achieve this by moving scalewise, in intervals of a second, in addition to calling the ear's attention by moving twice as fast as anything else in the context. Imagine how different their effect might be if these notes were to move just as quickly while circumscribing triads instead.

The sixteenths habitually initiate their motion from the second note of a four-note group, the first notes being tied to whatever preceded them in all but four cases: the first beats of bars 5, 10, 11, and 23. This type of motion nudges the ear off the downbeat on which it might otherwise have reposed.

QUESTION 3: Will you say a word to clarify the right-hand ornaments at measures 11, 13, and 19?

ANSWER 3: Let me answer in reverse order, because of the various levels of complexity. The ornament at bar 19 is merely a tied trill, of which you have surely heard enough by now. At bar 13 you have undoubtedly seen a threat to proper execution of the mordent in that the F-natural to which it would ordinarily descend, given the key signature, is already being sounded by the left hand. The simplest solution would be to use an F-sharp in the right-hand mordent thus: instead of

The notation of the right-hand trill at bar 11 (ex. 2.15) is more problematic. Much as it represents a typical tied trill procedure, the trill-note is identical to that to which it is bound by the tie (A-natural), not a step or half-step below it. This is very rare in the Partitas, although you will see it again. Perhaps you would like to view it as a slip of the pen, or as an indication of a trill upward from the A to B-flat. It is difficult to make a ruling in this case.

Example 2.15. Courante, bar 11, right hand

Sarabande

QUESTION 1: The radical contrast between this Sarabande and that of Partita I makes me wonder if I have turned the wrong page. Worse, it arouses doubt whether there is such a thing as a "sarabande" at all. How much more of this sort of thing is to be expected?

A N S W E R 1: Quite a good deal. The very history of the sarabande since its allegedly Spanish origins has proved it capable of dismaying transformations. Sarabandes began centuries ago as fast dances, often considered sensual and redolent with sin. Miguel de Cervantes, no mean vulgarian himself when so inclined, saw fit to condemn sarabandes as lascivious. There are even historical references, one hopes exaggerated, of people being sentenced to the galleys for dancing sarabandes as they were then perceived. The sarabande arrived at the French court by the end of the sixteenth century, still clothed in its reputation for voluptuousness. Only its endorsement by Cardinal Richelieu catapulted it into respectability.

Knowing the dance as it appears in Bach's suites, it seems out of the question to associate it with wickedness or sensuality. It is just possible, however, that some awareness of the sarabande's turbulent origins will help prepare one for the protean characterizations that Bach imposed upon it. It is easy to see the challenge they presented to a conscientious composer, if only by virtue of their comparative slowness, always a problem to contend with in pieces written for the harpsichord. How is one to compose a movement—usually the slowest in pulse of an entire suite—in ternary meter that is capable of producing a certain gravity on the second of three beats (and sometimes also the third) but does not cause its listeners to die of boredom? Only the greatest composers, Bach and Couperin most prominent among them, have met this challenge successfully. Some of the compositional devices used to solve this problem will be discussed in their turn, since the sarabandes in the six Partitas alone provide a display of wizardry.

Q U E S T I O N 2: Recalling Couperin's broad classification of sarabandes into *grave* and *tendre,* I gather that the present Sarabande is of the tendre type.

Example 2.16. Sarabande, bars 7–8

ANSWER 2: Yes, but in your search for clues to characterization, do not overlook certain reflections of string music similar to those mentioned in connection with the Allemande. Indeed, one might imagine the right-hand part being played on a violin and the left-hand part on a cello, although the two four-note chords in example 2.16 would then seem anticontextual.

QUESTION 3: Measures 17 through 19 seem to induce the same bogged-down feeling that I recall from bars 21 to 25 in the Allemande.

ANSWER 3: The pattern of two right-hand sixteenth notes against one left-hand eighth note is a sure invitation to trouble on the harpsichord, as you know from the passage in the Allemande. When the bass motion changes direction and the pace of harmonic change is altered in measure 20, your bogged-down feeling disappears. The solution is similar to that suggested for the Allemande: contrive a "ghost tune" by holding over certain notes, as illustrated in example 2.17.

Example 2.17. Sarabande, bars 17–19, right hand, altered to illustrate "ghost tune"

Rondeaux

QUESTION 1: Is the principal characteristic of rondo form a periodic return to a musical statement or section first heard at the very beginning?

ANSWER 1: Yes, and it is therefore regarded as the paragon of cyclic forms. It had its origin in French poetry but was soon taken up by musicians, who could not fail to appreciate the dynamic possibilities of this sort of pre-planned reiteration. The word *rondeau* properly refers only to the repeated statement, the musical areas with which it alternates being called *couplets*.

QUESTION 2: After the relatively slow Sarabande, a mischievous intuition tempts me to play this movement very fast.

ANSWER 2: Try for a speed record if you wish. My guess is that you will regret it at latest shortly after the second couplet has begun, perhaps at about measure 55. This movement has many ways of ensuring itself against stampeding. I will mention only a few and your own perceptions will provide the rest.

1. Look again at your left hand and remember your friend the continuo cellist.

2. Consider the syncopated right-hand notes, such as those at bars 18 to 21 (ex. 2.18).

Example 2.18. Rondeaux, bars 18–21

Harmonic changes occur beneath these syncopations. Any speed so highly propelled as to prevent them from being heard properly is too fast.

3. Similarly, in bars 3 to 6 (ex. 2.19), if you cannot hear the rests in their exact proportions, your speed is trampling these galvanic silences out of the music. Use them as guides to tempo instead.

Example 2.19. Rondeaux, bars 3–6

4. Another device for controlling speed is to use what might be called a slight portamento touch in the first measure and parallel situations. Lift your hand slightly for each of the three eighth notes instead of striking the high C and stretching your hand downward to traverse the octave, as you might otherwise do. This is bound to restrain speed, and it can add welcome gravity to the rondeau subject.

5. A jumble is created from bar 55 to about bar 60 by an astonishing metrical displacement. If you are playing too fast the effect of this will be lost, and that is fatal.

6. The right-hand triplets at bars 86 and 87 (ex. 2.20) pose similar problems. At excessive speed you will be unable either to execute them as music or to negotiate them at all.

Example 2.20. Rondeaux, bars 86–87

QUESTION 3: The decorative figure on the third beat of bar 82, right hand (ex. 2.21), is often made to sound like a triplet. I presume that this cannot be literally correct.

Example 2.21. Rondeaux, bar 82, right hand

ANSWER 3: It is absolutely wrong. Excessive speed is a major cause of unauthorized "tripletizing."

QUESTION 4: The small-note appoggiatura in bar 83 is often heard as a very short note. What if a player decides that a short appoggiatura sounds intrusive and injects too much "snap" into a cantabile passage? Is he allowed to make it longer?

ANSWER 4: From your general knowledge of appoggiaturas, you must know that the answer is yes. The player is then responsible, however, for adjusting the fingering. The main thing to remember is that such appoggiaturas move to their notes of resolution by legato motion, for which the fingering must provide.

QUESTION 5: I have been saving this question for the last. The ornament on the third right-hand eighth note (ex. 2.22) is positively embarrassing! I cannot think of it as anything but a tongue-twister, and I certainly cannot make it sound as if it belonged there.

Example 2.22. Rondeaux, bars 1–2

ANSWER 5: This ornament has always been controversial. In the Bach table of ornaments the item that most closely resembles it is the Doppelt-Cadence. If this is true, then the realization of the symbol is

Whether or not we so define it, it is surely a trill with a prefix from below. Perhaps the most useful answer to your question will be to paraphrase the arguments for and against omitting the ornament, keeping in mind that no conclusions will result to satisfy everyone.

1. *For:* The ornament appears only in bar 1 and is never seen again.

Against: A good argument but not decisive. The cyclic form leads us to expect the repetitions of the rondeau sections to incorporate all their principal characteristics. The ornament might have been expected whether notated or not.

2. *For:* The awkwardness of this ornament in bar 1 is multiplied tenfold if it is attempted in the left hand, which enters in otherwise exactly canonical imitation.

Against: Granted. In that case leave it out of the left hand, where it is not indicated anyway.

3. *For:* The ornament's "prefix," judging this to be the note C, has been heard immediately before, and the main body of the trill involves a rising second, a particularly graceless situation.

Against: Again granted, but not decisive. There are many examples of such ornament progressions in this repertoire.

4. *For:* Among modern editions both Bischoff and the older Bachgesellschaft print an unprefixed trill. Even then Bischoff declares it in a footnote to be "highly questionable."*

*J. S. Bach, *Six Partitas and Overture in French Style,* ed. Hans Bischoff (1882, reprint, New York, 1942), 24*n*1.

Example 2.23. Rondeaux, bar 73, with ornament

Against: Nonsense. The ornament is a Doppelt-Cadence in all sources.
5. *For:* The ornament sounds outright disagreeable at bar 73 (ex. 2.23).
Against: Very simple: do not play it at bar 73.

Capriccio

QUESTION 1: Is this the only time the gigue is omitted in the major Bach suite collections?

ANSWER 1: If you are asking whether all the French and English Suites, as well as every partita but this one, incorporate a gigue, the answer is yes. The "Overture in the French Manner" in *Clavier-Übung* contains a gigue, but not as the final movement. To us this change in the customary position of the gigue seems exceptional, but there is ample precedent in the suites of some of Bach's predecessors and even in his own orchestral Suites.

Moreover, your distress at the omission of a final gigue here should be mitigated by the degree to which the Capriccio succeeds as a substitute. For example, the Capriccio benefits from fugal treatment of dazzling ingenuity—a cherished ingredient in some of Bach's best gigues. It also conducts itself formally very much as a fugal gigue would, establishing the tonality of the dominant at mid-part and driving homeward to the tonic during the second half. The magnificent contrivance of inverting the subject in this second part is observed, and even the reminiscence of the theme right-side-up (a regular item in Bach's fugal gigues) is provided at bar 87 in the left hand (ex. 2.24).

Example 2.24. Capriccio, bar 87

If you add to the above some understanding of the character of the piece, a chugging-along type of motion, highly animated, always grounded and never breezy, one wonders what is left to miss of a gigue except its title.

QUESTION 2: What is this talk about "chugging along" and "never breezy"? A serious piece of music is being discussed, not harness-racing.

ANSWER 2: I hoped the imaginative terminology would draw your fire. "Chugging along" was intended to convey that, although the movement does not lack considerable wit and liveliness, both the nature of the subject and the leaping motion scattered throughout discredit the frequent treatment of this movement as a frivolous addendum to a long and occasionally melodramatic partita. "Never breezy" suggests a certain heavy-handedness dictated by the musical symptoms mentioned in Answer 1 and too seldom audible at the unhinged speeds which often bruise this Capriccio in modern performances.

QUESTION 3: Can the leaps beyond octave range be construed as further allusions to string writing? They seem unusual among Bach's harpsichord works but are one of the principal characteristics of this movement from their first appearance in bar 3 (ex. 2.25).

Example 2.25. Capriccio, bar 3, right hand

Example 2.26, Concerto in D minor for two violins, Allegro, bars 21–23, solo part

ANSWER 3: I would say so. It may amuse you to know that commentators have often compared this feature of the Capriccio with the Concerto in D minor for two violins (ex. 2.26), written somewhat earlier in Bach's career.

QUESTION 4: Is it, then, this allusion to string music that causes hazards to the keyboard player? I seem to have heard that song before.

A N S W E R 4: Technical problems in traversing larger-than-octave spaces may well result from dealing with a resource not typically found in harpsichord music this side of Domenico Scarlatti. We might call it "rebound action." Understanding this term to mean bouncing off point A to reach point B, let me offer a few hints applicable to this Capriccio.

Most music of this period is written so that at almost any given moment the majority of forthcoming notes lie within the compass of the hand. This extends to about one octave when the hand is in its native habitat and not displaced into some foreign range of the keyboard. In bar 3, however, you must traverse intervals of a tenth.

At first you may delude yourself into thinking you have a choice between *stretching* your hand for the traversal or *leaping,* by pushing or bouncing off the first note in the direction of the second. You will soon find that you have no such choice. A leap—that is, a movement of the forearm transferring the hand from one keyboard area to another—will be your only answer. Remember that if you try to leap and stretch at the same time, you vastly increase your chances of missing.

In deciding to leap you must be aware of where the hand has been during most of its recent activity—in other words, where it has arrived by finger action before the leap. In bar 3 the area around the first E-flat is the right hand's homeland at the moment. The note it must land on is the second note, the high G. If trouble comes, it is likely to be there. Knowing which end of the leap holds greater hazards is vital to proper practicing. If this seems nitpicking, play the whole measure and consciously assess the difference in sensation between your leap away from the first to the second note and your return home between the second and third notes. Although the length of the second leap is greater, almost no problems exist because the hand is returning. Knowing which end of the leap harbors the dangers will cut your anxieties in half. In this Capriccio in particular you should also be aware that a leap away from the body holds more inherent technical problems than does a leap toward it.

Example 2.27. Capriccio, bars 51–52

QUESTION 5: You have stated that one has no choice here between stretching and leaping. I think, however, that I have found a situation in the second half of the Capriccio where leaping cannot possibly be managed. Let me have your comments on bar 52 (ex. 2.27).

ANSWER 5: I must of course concede that a leap in the left hand is impossible here. The problem is caused mainly by the downward-stemming of the bass E-flat into a quarter note. A stretch seems required, but, because it is awkward, it has often been suggested that the value of the E-flat should not be taken literally. Although this conjecture is clearly defensive, players cite two points in favor of considering the quarter note a slip of the pen. The first, and to me the less valid, is that in the previous measure the bass line marched along quite satisfactorily in eighth notes. The second argument holds that on many other occasions involving note values Bach seems to have been careful to liberate players' hands for new tasks. The eighth-note value of the B-natural on the first beat of bar 60 is cited (ex. 2.28).

Example 2.28. Capriccio, bars 59–60, left hand

Whether or not we credit such arguments, the situation at bar 52 does not present quite the same problem as do the skips of tenths in, say, measure 3. Bar 52 offers more than mere sound effect or technical challenge: it is the entrance of the inverted subject in the bass in a highly concentrated fugal treatment. This places it in a special category. The problem ceases to be merely technical and musical considerations must take precedence over rebound techniques, notational imprecisions, and all other accessories that, after all, can only operate in the service of a musical result.

PARTITA III

Fantasia

QUESTION 1: May we start, as usual, with the title?

ANSWER 1: This movement was originally called "Prelude" in Anna Magdalena's *Notebook*. You will observe that Bach merely exchanged one nondescript title for another. In fact, many of the comments made about the word *praeludium* in Partita I apply equally to the fantasia, a term which embraces such divergent musical organisms as the *Chromatic Fantasia,* the binary-form Fantasia in C minor, and the Three-Part Inventions or Sinfonias, as they came to be called.

It is misleading to associate the fantasia with our word *fantastic,* implying strange or bizarre. The *Chromatic Fantasia* may fit that description, but the Three-Part Inventions, for all their expressive beauty and variety, are strict contrapuntal exercises—hardly the proper vehicle for musical ripping and snorting. The same holds true for this Fantasia, which is a highly distilled and extended essay in two-part writing.

You may well ask why Bach used "fantasia" in the 1731 version of the Partitas. Would not "prelude" have served the same purpose? The best answer seems to be that he had already written a "praeludium" in Partita I and a "praeambulum" was forthcoming in Partita V; to call another opening movement "prelude" might have been viewed as incompatible with his intention of endowing each such movement with a different title, a feature unique to the six Partitas.

QUESTION 2: However one views this Fantasia, it seems to present more dangers for the performer than the familiar Two-Part Inventions. For example, a harpsichordist can easily be taken aback by the endless flow of sixteenth notes. In the Inventions the thematic material seems more shapely, better punctuated metrically, and thus endowed with more tangible contours.

ANSWER 2: What you describe as an "endless flow" of sixteenth notes has bothered you before. This movement, however, is much more than a continuous stream of sixteenth notes. The subject is stated in the right hand of bar 1, beginning with a sixteenth-note rest that is itself part of the thematic "shape." The bass moves in simple continuo accompaniment, incorporating a syncopation between the last eighth note of bar 1 and the first of bar 2, and the right hand moves in eighth notes in bars 3 and 4.

Perhaps the length of the movement disturbs you. Or you may be distressed by the succession of sixteenth notes because you do not fully understand the musical shapes within those passages. Let me suggest a few questions you might ask yourself in order to grasp the phrase structure of the piece:

1. In what keys are the measures couched in example 3.1—that is, what is the prevailing tonality of each measure, taken independently of its neighbors?

Example 3.1. Fantasia, bars 9–11

2. Which are the nonchord tones and how do they create friction with the tonality you have determined to be predominant?

3. Which notes hover around a central point and which depart from it by measurably larger intervallic traversals? Singers and nonkeyboard players would need to be concerned about this. So do you, particularly in such sparsely textured music.

4. Try singing the right- or left-hand notes in example 3.1 or other sections of the Fantasia. This will impress on you the *direction* of the intervals far more effectively than merely depressing keys on a keyboard. Now explain to yourself the *sizes* of the intervals and how many move successively in the same direction.

5. Are there groups of three or more consecutive notes that would form a simple chord, such as a triad or any of its inversions, if played simultaneously?

Because these preliminary study procedures may seem somewhat harrowing, faced as you are with 120 measures of antiseptic two-part writing, I think it only fitting to proffer some consolation. In much of this Fantasia you can invite the assistance of our old friend, the imaginary continuo player. In measures 21 to 30 (ex. 3.2), you will, in fact, not be able to do without him. Simply assure yourself that he knows how to phrase, and take care that he does not blow you out of your seat with downbeats!

Example 3.2. Fantasia, bars 21–30, with phrasing indications

The fact that the Fantasia is pervaded by sequences means that should any mishap occur, it will inevitably sound like a disaster. But sequences also make the performer's work easier, since once you have devised a successful scheme of phrasing and articulation, it can be applied repeatedly throughout the movement.

QUESTION 3: What about tempo? I use the word in its broadest sense, meaning speed of performance or pulse. It is difficult to isolate any feature in this Fantasia that might provide a dependable clue.

ANSWER 3: If you apply the practice suggestions I have just made, you will find yourself well provided with signposts. Among other things, you will notice that excessive speed will obscure some of the musical features alluded to in Answer 2. On the other hand, playing too slowly will make the music sound charmless and heavy-footed. If you listen carefully, your speed, properly derived from musical sources, should eventually attain focus.

QUESTION 4: Extended sections of the Fantasia consist of sixteenth notes in the right hand played against eighth notes in the left. We have discussed the possible dangers of this before, but I remember previous occasions as being more sporadic and less prevalent in movements characterized by imitations between the hands.

ANSWER 4: If the phrasing of the sixteenth notes, wherever they appear, is well wrought, it will almost unfailingly disallow any two-against-one monotony. Moreover, the correct phrasing of the eighth notes will emerge naturally from an understanding of their continuo characteristics. Rigorously observing the bar lines in measures 21 to 31, for example, will produce a static effect, however comfortable it may be to play. But if you make slightly greater demands on the musicality of your continuo player, as indicated by the brackets in example 3.2, you will come a long way toward providing independence of parts, thereby giving musical shape to the succession of eighth notes. This, in turn will insure against the stultifying two-against-one syndrome.

QUESTION 5: Can you comment on the ornaments in this movement? Few of them are represented by symbols and the editions presently in use contain many discrepancies.

ANSWER 5: In list form:

1. Bar 52, right hand: a tied trill between the first and second notes.
2. Bar 54, right hand: an ordinary trill on the dotted-quarter F-sharp.
3. Bar 65, right hand: Henle prints ⌇⌇, presumably suggesting an ordinary trill from above with a slight additional emphasis or prolongation of the initial upper note. At the virtually identical situation in bar 96, however, the symbol is ⌇⌇ . The rounded form of the trill prefix indicates a Doppelt-Cadence from above, according to Bach's ornament table in the *Clavier-Büchlein*. It is difficult to ascertain why this distinction is made in modern print. The earlier version of this movement in Anna Magdalena's *Notebook* yields no revelations at all.
4. Bars 101 and 102, right hand: upper appoggiaturas preceding the first note of each measure. These ornaments are found only in Henle 1979, their source being copies of a second edition of unknown date in the British Library

and the Library of Congress. Their authority derives from several additions to the text that are suspected to be in Bach's own hand.

Allemande

QUESTION 1: I understand that "speed" in performance can be logically derived from "tempo," that is, from the inward activity of a movement. However, the opposite assumption—that arbitrarily superimposed "speed" is a reliable guide to a movement's inner workings—is far less likely to be true. I have applied this principle successfully before, but in this Allemande the pulse again eludes me. There seem to be no lofty images, no edifying allusions to the sound of string instruments or anything of the kind. The piece is quite playable technically, yet refuses to stand and fight. Comparison to the Allemandes in Partitas I and II generates nothing but an aggravated perplexity.

ANSWER 1: You may be surprised to learn that Thoinot Arbeau had already pronounced the allemande obsolete as a dance in 1588, in a treatise on dancing entitled *Orchésographie*. If, notwithstanding this, allemandes continue to appear in suites of later times, we may safely assume that composers were more concerned with their musical value than with their choreographic origins.

Since you are obviously trying to arrive at your answers in the proper way, I will take the risk of invoking a more nebulous dimension of the learning process. All of us who have attempted to improvise continuo accompaniments are aware that there is such a thing as "finger wisdom," a mysterious force born of keyboard experience that occasionally gets us into and out of trouble at times when premeditation and brain power are not given time to intervene. The truly formidable exploiters of this wisdom are the great jazz pianists, by far the most creative continuo players of all time. This wisdom may easily teach you more about the tempo, and therefore about the speed, of the Allemande than all the harmonic analyses and theoretical ruminations you could possibly bring to bear on it.

In any case, I agree with you that comparing this movement to previous allemandes in the Partitas, even for the purpose of establishing contrasts rather than kinships, is very nearly the worst move you could have made. You must look instead to the dotted rhythms that pervade this movement. The Allemande is a veritable etude in dotted motion. As a matter of fact, when Bach revised the Partitas for publication in 1731, he made dotting unavoidable in some places where it had not been specified in the *Notebook* of Anna Magdalena (exx. 3.3 and 3.4).

Example 3.3. Allemande, bar 2, right hand, Anna Magdalena version

Example 3.4. Allemande, bar 2, right hand, 1731 version

QUESTION 2: If I may bring up a controversial subject, advocates of universal double-dotting or over-dotting cannot seem to resist temptation when any of the following appears: (a) a long note followed by a short note; (b) a series of notes written ♩. ♬ and interpreted as ♩. ♬; or (c) a rest followed by a short note, in which the rest is regarded as the long note in a long-short combination. Judging by these guidelines, the first beat in bar 7, right hand (ex. 3.5), seems to present a problem.

Example 3.5. Allemande, bars 6–7

As I hear it, this figure represents the second step in a sequence initiated on the last beat of bar 6. The latter is notated ♩ ♬♬. ♪, a rhythmic pattern that brings double-dotting to mind immediately. The first beat of bar 7, on the other hand, consists of notes of equal value, the first of which is not tied to any previous incident. A failure to treat both figures in the same way will damage the sequence.

ANSWER 2: Double-dotting is a matter of taste. A musical sequence is a matter of fact and must take precedence.

52

QUESTION 3: What is the verdict on double-dotting the upbeat measure to the first half of the Allemande (ex. 3.6)?

Example 3.6. Allemande, beginning

ANSWER 3: Partisans of over-dotting point to the mordent on the right-hand E, which does not exist in the Anna Magdalena version. They claim that the mordent calls the listener to attention so successfully after the sobrieties of the Fantasia that it (or some other device accomplishing the same purpose) must have been played, whether notated or not. By animating the comparatively long E, over-dotting enhances the ensuing outburst of radically fore-shortened notes.

In the left-hand part of this same measure, the over-dotting constituency cites the initial sixteenth-note rest as providing the necessary license. They compare it to the arpeggios in bars 2 and 3 of the left hand, which seem to respond to execution as sixty-fourth notes instead of the written thirty-seconds. No one claims that the situations are identical, but the principle is the same, since all three arpeggio figurations begin with a rest that can be regarded as the long element in a long-short combination. Thus, the third of the conditions outlined in Question 2 is, according to some, clearly fulfilled.

QUESTION 4: Am I correct in assuming that double-dotting will cause the three encircled notes in example 3.7 to sound simultaneously? And are these notes aligned with each other in the 1731 edition?

Example 3.7. Allemande, bar 6

ANSWER 4: Yes, double-dotting will cause these three notes to coincide. They are indeed almost perfectly aligned in the sources. Incidentally, the ornament on the G-natural in the right hand of measure 6 is called a *Doppelt-Cadence und Mordant* in the Bach ornament table, where its realization is given as

In Anna Magdalena's *Notebook,* the ornament  appears over the same G-natural. This combination of symbols is familiar in the music of, for example, François Couperin, where it usually indicates a trill terminating in a turn:

In his 1731 revision, however, Bach turned the Anna Magdalena ornament backwards and upside-down. A "hook" appears at the beginning of the trill, obviously dissociating it from any terminating function. Furthermore, the hook depicts motion upward to the ornamented note from its lower neighbor, instead of downward from its upper neighbor. This leaves the mordent (indicated by the vertical slash at the end of the trill symbol itself) to provide the termination. The notation ⌇ never occurs again in the six Partitas, either in the Anna Magdalena version of Partitas III and VI or in the 1731 compilation.

QUESTION 5: At the end of the first and second sections of the Allemande (ex. 3.8), a pianist could achieve a diminuendo quite easily between the

Example 3.8. Allemande, bars 8 and 16

penultimate eighth-note chord and its resolution. Assuming the idea to be stylistically acceptable, can a harpsichordist approximate this effect, and if so, how?

ANSWER 5: Of course the idea is acceptable. This is simply another clear case of organic dynamics. Observe that in both of the above cadences the music moves from a fairly dense texture on the first half of the beat to a thinner one on the second half. In bar 16 the low octave in the left hand evokes additional resonance from the harpsichord. Since more notes almost inevitably produce a stronger sound, organic diminuendo is guaranteed. The prolonged quarter notes B in bar 8 and E in bar 16 further subdue the attack of the second cadential chords by virtue of their overhanging resonance.

Remember that appoggiaturas tend to be resolved by legato motion. Well executed, this legato will enhance the diminuendo effect. Notice that the harmony on both semifinal chords is sufficiently dissonant to demand a resolution and that the tritones must resolve by half-steps. The slur in bar 8 helps to insure a smooth transition between the cadential chords. The omission of this slur at bar 16 makes little difference. A legato marking at either of these two points only confirms what anyone with a drop of musical sense would do anyway.

Corrente

QUESTION 1: The prefix to the trill on D-natural in bar 17 (ex. 3.9) is written out in thirty-second notes. Why did Bach not use the Doppelt-Cadence symbol ∿ , as illustrated in his own ornament table? This would seem to have accomplished the same thing.

Example 3.9. Corrente, bar 17

ANSWER 1: Had the prefix-plus-trill been depicted by the symbol you suggest, the ornament would probably have been played on the beat. Bach seems to have wanted the prefix to anticipate the D-natural. His intention is confirmed by the notation of the same ornament in Anna Magdalena's *Notebook*, where the prefix is written in sixteenth notes. It is obviously meant to be played before the D-natural, although it is not preceded (as in example 3.9) by a dotted note or any of the other standard invitations to double-dotting which, in the view of some, might cause the two prefix notes to be pushed forward almost into the second beat of the measure.

As for the written-out termination, I am sure you have noticed that the left hand moves parallel to the right from the second beat of bar 17 into bar 18. (This is equally true in the Anna Magdalena version.) Bach might have sought to insure perfect synchronization between hands by writing out the trill terminations. Remember that they do not necessarily need to be played exactly as sixteenth notes. Whatever you do, however, make certain that the terminations are perfectly synchronized. To do otherwise would be disastrous.

Q U E S T I O N 2: I cannot help hearing an intensification of sound (I take it I am not to use the word *crescendo*!) starting at about measure 37 and expanding gradually to what seems a culmination at measure 42 (ex. 3.10). Does this classify me as a musical outcast who listens to Bach with self-deluding, post-Wagnerian ears?

Example 3.10. Corrente, bars 37–42

A N S W E R 2: Hardly. The Corrente contains a good deal of that sort of thing—for example, in bars 5 and 6, and 25 to about 28. As you consider this passage keep these points in mind:

1. The tonal plane rises stepwise, but not so gradually that your ear loses the relationship between one stage and the next. Psychologists tell us that controlled rises in pitch register mounting agitation.

2. The figuration is insistent and repetitive.

3. Given the usual pulse requirements of correntes, the speed is by no

means slow. Thus, the cumulative impact of the characteristics described above can be all the more easily heard and felt.

All of the above, as well as other features you may discover for yourself, contribute to the illusion of crescendo, without a literal increase in loudness. If pedantic academicians disallow the word *crescendo*, then invent your own name for it, but do not deny that it is in the music.

Sarabande

Q U E S T I O N 1: The ornament on the second eighth note in the upbeat measure seems to intrude on the natural melodic flow, particularly at the slow speed of a sarabande. Since the ornament occurs throughout the movement, would you care to comment?

A N S W E R 1: The ornament ⌇ is called a *Trillo und Mordant* in the Bach table, and its execution here and in all parallel situations is as follows (ex. 3.11):

Example 3.11. Realization of *Trillo und Mordant*

Notice the F-sharp. Although this is not provided for in the key signature or indicated by any other means of notation, an F-natural as the lower note of the termination would be unthinkable. Executing the ornament so that it does not exceed the duration of the note to which the symbol pertains provides the perfect literal rendition. This prevents the note immediately after the ornament (in this case, A-natural) from sounding as if it were incorporated in the symbol.

Opponents of this interpretation are quick to argue that (a) the deciphering of the symbol for the *Trillo und Mordant* in Bach's table does not literally demand any differences in note value in the component notes of the ornament; and (b) that the version in example 3.11 can become rather clumsy to play in certain passages.

Be careful of editors like Bischoff who recognize this ornament as their old friend the "inverted mordent," leaving the termination to the performer's discretion, or other editions that identify it as a *Pralltriller* with a termination. The latter in particular is like saying that when your aunt wears trousers, she becomes your uncle.

Perhaps this would be a good time to clarify the confusion caused by the terms *Pralltriller, inverted mordent,* and *Schneller.* A Pralltriller, often called a "half-trill," is a variant of the tremblement lié or tied trill. It is played very quickly and, according to Friedrich Wilhelm Marpurg, usually consists of only three notes. C. P. E. Bach regards it as invariably pursuing a downward and stepwise motion (ex. 3.12).

Example 3.12. Notation and realization of *Pralltriller* by C. P. E. Bach

The other two ornaments are virtually identical, except that the Schneller is not necessarily approached by a descending second. It can involve a leap from almost anywhere, as you can see in Marpurg's famous example (ex. 3.13):

Example 3.13. Realization of *Schneller,* from Marpurg's *Anleitung zum Clavierspielen* (1755)

The Schneller is written out, usually in small notes, and not represented by any symbol or abbreviation.

QUESTION 2: At bar 22 (ex. 3.14), two sixteenth notes in the right hand occur simultaneously with a sixteenth-note triplet in the left. What would have been the most likely reading of this apparent two-against-three figure in Bach's time, and how should it be performed today?

Example 3.14. Sarabande, bar 22

ANSWER 2: There is considerable evidence that dotted motion would have been imposed on the duple rhythm of the right hand, so that the second of the two right-hand notes would coincide with the third note of the left-hand triplet. This solution can be and frequently is challenged, however, and must not be taken as an iron-clad law. Again, context must be taken into account. If, for example, two moving parts each contain material of independent and equal thematic importance, resorting to dotted motion to accommodate a concurrent triplet might damage a thematic statement. In this case, the two-against-three juxtaposition would have to be played as written and considered a feature of the polyphonic picture.

Another commonsense suggestion is that the right-hand E on the first beat of bar 22 is a natural place for a trill. In this case, the two succeeding sixteenth notes could be regarded as a trill termination and the player could place them wherever he wished, within reason, thereby avoiding the two-against-three issue entirely. This is worth attempting at your own risk, but be warned that no trill indication appears on the E in question in any properly accredited source, from Anna Magdalena's *Notebook* to the 1731 revision.

QUESTION 3: The Anna Magdalena version notates the first beat of measure 8 this way (ex. 3.15):

Example 3.15. Sarabande, bar 8, right hand, Anna Magdalena version

The upturned slash between the C and E on the first eighth note clearly indicates some ornamental device which does not appear in many editions and is not accounted for in the Bach ornament table. Can you explain what this slash means and why it appears only in the *Notebook* of Anna Magdalena?

ANSWER 3: The slash is a fairly common device which you will encounter again on several crucial occasions in Partita VI. It indicates that you should play the D between the C and E, but release it immediately to allow the major third to sound. Thus, the execution is something like

This ornament interjects a dissonant note and forces you to roll the third upward, instead of playing it exactly as written.

Although no such ornament appears in the Bach table, François Couperin calls it a *tierce coulée* and d'Anglebert a *coulé sur une tierce*. The 1731 source is extremely difficult to read at this point, owing to blotching and blurring, and attempts to decipher Bach's intentions have remained inconclusive through many sunrises in the taverns of the calligraphic mind. Among modern editions, Henle 1979 seems to favor

while Bischoff prefers the following (obviously in deference to the Anna Magdalena version):

QUESTION 4: Once more I have the feeling that Bach is asking me to play music that the harpsichord will never really let me hear. Since this problem has arisen several times previously, I wonder what you might have to say about its resurgence in this movement.

ANSWER 4: My guess is that you have been put off by too much detailed discussion of the ornaments. Isolated from the music itself, they tend to seem like intrusive villains. This is partially to blame for the incongruity you feel between the natural cantabile expression of this Sarabande and the ornamental artifices, which can sound like fire alarms in the middle of a lullaby if they are not thoroughly mastered. Do not forget that composers often relied upon ornamentation in sarabandes, not only because slow-moving music provided the ideal opportunity for such decorations, but also because embellishments helped compensate for the harpsichord's acoustical shortcomings. With that in mind, here are a few suggestions:

1. Think of this Sarabande as a type of song with accompaniment. Do not allow yourself to be intimidated by the apparent imitation between the outer voices in bar 1. This is not a contrapuntal work.

2. Make sure not to rush the triplets. If you do, the basically slow pulse will make the resulting disorder especially offensive. Avoiding heaviness on the first note of each triplet is a useful technique for achieving proper control.

3. Do not allow the ornaments to cause any breaches of pulse. The recurrence of the difficult Trillo und Mordant figure is a potential source of danger.

The mordents (such as that on the first E in the right hand) should be very quick, barely allowing the lower component to be heard. Playing them with heavenly languor will totally change their relationship to the notes that follow. This is corroborated in bar 17 (ex. 3.16), where Bach elects to change that relationship and therefore adopts an entirely different notation.

Example 3.16. Sarabande, bar 17, right hand

4. On whatever harpsichord you use, select a lyrical, unincisive registration. The overall sound should be pliable rather than trenchant. Beware of couplings of any sort. These may aggravate the keyboard action and cause you to emphasize the very crispness of attack you are attempting to avoid.

5. Hold every note down as long as possible, releasing it only when necessary to insure the clarity of the following note. This will seem especially difficult in some of the repeated-note passages in the left hand. As I have said before in other contexts, it will help to think of cello bowings or vocal syllables that do not end in sharp consonant sounds. You are never likely to find the results completely satisfactory, but trying to play this Sarabande without observing any of the above suggestions is like looking through the wrong end of a telescope.

Burlesca

QUESTION 1: Our venerated Thuringian father really seems to have chosen a fanciful title this time!

ANSWER 1: The Italian word *burla* denotes something intended to provoke laughter, usually by distortion or exaggeration. It is not, however, synonymous with "parody." Benedetto Marcello's *Teatro alla moda* of 1720, for example, is an uproarious parody of opera, but it is not "burlesque." The latter involves humor of a much coarser fabric, tends to insult its subject, and traditionally seems more prone to unabashed vulgarity.

In the earlier version of Partita III in Anna Magdalena's *Notebook*, the present movement is entitled "Menuet," that is, a dance for two, with three beats to the measure, usually associated with the very height of courtliness. Yet there are no major changes between it and the finished product of 1731. In fact, the movement always contained undertones of the piquant and grotesque in its occasional awkwardness and deliberately stilted and graceless gestures. Such characteristics are not usually expected in minuets of this period. (Please keep in mind that the more emancipated minuets of the classical period, such as one finds in the music of Joseph Haydn, are a totally different matter.) It may be, therefore, that Bach really intended to call the movement a "burlesca" from the start and that the earlier title "menuet" was imposed for reasons not strictly concerned with the nature of the musical expression.

QUESTION 2: What is the meaning of the dots above the second and third beats of bars 5 and 6 (ex. 3.17)? Are they authentic and, if so, how should they be viewed by the performer?

Example 3.17. Burlesca, bars 5–6, right hand

ANSWER 2: The dots are indeed in the 1731 sources, though not in the Anna Magdalena version. This notation is extremely rare and, in this instance, difficult to interpret. It does not seem likely that the dots are merely staccato indications, since this would make absolutely no sense on the third beat of bar 22, which is tied to the succeeding note. An explanation frequently propounded is that the dots pertain to clavichord performance. Even more popular and equally untenable is the theory that they demand a strong accent from the harpsichordist. At this one's head merely goes around in circles. I'm afraid I cannot give the answer your question deserves. But should you wish to forage further in the Partitas in search of clues, look at measures 1 and 5 of the Menuet of Partita IV, and measure 23 of the Corrente of Partita V. Both passages will be dealt with in due course.

QUESTION 3: Should the two sixteenth notes following the trills in measure 1 (ex. 3.18) and elsewhere be viewed as a little more important than mere terminations?

Example 3.18. Burlesca, bar 1, right hand

ANSWER 3: I firmly believe that a good deal of the drollery in this movement is inherent in these two sixteenths when played exactly as written. In so doing, moreover, you will find it easier to obtain perfect synchronization when the figure appears in both hands simultaneously, as in measure 17.

On the other hand, should you prefer a less strict observance of these exact note values, you may cite measure 9 (ex. 3.19) as evidence of some leniency in the matter on Bach's part.

Example 3.19. Burlesca, bar 9

Among the things you must *not* do is refer to measure 11 (ex. 3.20). Here the reason for forsaking the sixteenth-note values may be the uncomfortable consecutive ninths in the voice leading and have nothing to do with rhythmic considerations.

Example 3.20. Burlesca, bar 11

QUESTION 4: Between bars 33 and 37, do I hear another of those organic crescendi we talked about in the Corrente?

ANSWER 4: Yes.

QUESTION 5: Would it be very learned of me to attribute the descending octave unisons in measure 32 (ex. 3.21) to the influence of Vivaldi, or would this merely be futile name-dropping?

Example 3.21. Burlesca, bar 32

A N S W E R 5: This type of writing is extremely rare in Bach's harpsichord works, and it is quite understandable that commentators invariably want to say something about it. In fact, the late Glenn Gould felt an aversion to this entire partita because of measure 32. He claimed (only half in jest) that he could not believe his beloved Johann Sebastian could resort to such a pedestrian musical device as parallel octaves.

These unisons occur frequently in the concerted music of Vivaldi, Marcello, Geminiani, and other Italian composers. But the influence of Italian instrumental music on Bach ran far deeper and broader than any single "trick." You might consider how well suited an outburst like this is to the idea of a burlesca. Perhaps the sound-effect nature of the measure, with its empty-headed octaves, was intended as part of the joke. No one in his right mind would suggest that Bach wrote this passage because he could not think of anything else, as seems to have been the case with some of the resounding mediocrities of the Italian instrumental school.

Scherzo

Q U E S T I O N 1: Another surprising title!

A N S W E R 1: The more so because it follows the Burlesca. The Italian word *scherzo* means joke or jest. You may wonder what sort of frolicsome mood overtook Bach toward the end of a partita that began so soberly, and in the key of A minor at that. You should not, however, be surprised at the title "scherzo" merely because it is not, strictly speaking, the name of a dance movement, such as an allemande or a sarabande. You already have considerable experience with that sort of thing in the last two movements of Partita II and in the foregoing Burlesca.

Q U E S T I O N 2: In the upbeat measure, does not the heavy left-hand chord produce a seismic shock on the harpsichord? Should this chord be rolled or arpeggiated in some way?

ANSWER 2: Not on your life! There can be no softening of the blow this time. Notice how the dynamics are organized from the upbeat bar to the first beat of measure 2: first a chord of four notes, then three, then two, and finally a single note (ex. 3.22). Furthermore, the pattern is instantly repeated, hardly an invitation for the performer to tamper with it.

Example 3.22. Scherzo, beginning

QUESTION 3: What of the wild-eyed harmonic outcry at measures 28 and 29 (ex. 3.23)? Could Domenico Scarlatti have paid a surreptitious visit to Leipzig for which history has not accounted?

Example 3.23. Scherzo, bars 28–30

ANSWER 3: The incident is perfectly extraordinary in Bach and indeed reminiscent of Scarlatti's view of acciaccatura. The notation itself suggests the Scarlatti principle of regarding the dissonant note as an integral part of the chord's anatomy; there is no indication that the friction-creating G-sharp should be released any sooner than the other members of the chord on the second beat in measure 28. When Bach demands such an effect, as in bar 2 of the Toccata of Partita VI, his notation is altogether different.

QUESTION 4: I have heard the Burlesca and Scherzo performed in an "alternativamente" arrangement, as in Menuet I–Menuet II–Menuet I. Is this an accepted procedure?

ANSWER 4: No. The two movements are not recognized dance forms, and even if they are interpreted as dances masquerading under other names, the difference in meters is not characteristic of Bach's "alternativamente" juxtapositions. Furthermore, the Scherzo does not exist in the original version of this partita in Anna Magdalena's *Notebook*. Its insertion in the 1731 compilation is usually attributed to Bach's desire to have seven movements in each partita, although this conjecture is contradicted by the fact that Partita II comprises only six separately entitled movements.

Gigue

QUESTION 1: This movement, with its triplets cantering down the page and so on, looks very much as a gigue ought to look. Is some complexity escaping me?

ANSWER 1: There is no great complexity here, but, again, beware of being deceived by the visual image of the music. If you are tempted to regard this gigue as a trivial virtuoso vehicle, reread our remarks on triplets in the Corrente of Partita I. This will remind you that all triplets do not do the same thing. In this movement, some triplets outline a simple harmony, while others repeat themselves exactly, allowing the real activity to go on around them. Some incorporate ties that invalidate the visual impression of unremitting triplet motion. Still others encompass harmonic departures that make little rhetorical sense unless one thinks of them as interlocking to arrive at a point of resolution.

I would also draw your attention to the fact that this movement, like many Bach gigues, is organized fugally. That the subject is inverted after the central double bar will not surprise you, since you have already encountered this in the Capriccio of Partita II. Although you have seen a Bach movement in triplet motion ending a "suite" (the Giga of Partita I), you have not heretofore seen a final *fugal* movement composed of triplets. So much for the simple appearance of this Gigue on the printed page.

QUESTION 2: The movement begins with a single-note upbeat. Is this customary?

ANSWER 2: The Gigues of four of the English Suites and three of the French Suites begin with single-note upbeats. If you add to these the gigues of Partitas III and V, you may count nine of the seventeen gigues in Bach's major suites as starting in this fashion. Far more important than these raw statistics, however, is the immense force these upbeats exercise during the progress of the movements they initiate. For example, some introduce the proceedings with a melodic interval of a major or minor second. Other upbeat notes, as in the present Gigue, are further strengthened by their unmistakable invocation of dominant tonality. In the context of a fugal treatment, careful attention to these notes can provide the performer with a powerful weapon for clarifying the assorted entrances of the subject, as well as determining phrase-shapes. You may say that this applies to any upbeat note in any context. True, but in polyphonic situations these single upbeat notes are especially crucial to the performer's subsequent decisions.

Q U E S T I O N 3: In example 3.24, is the encircled note G-natural or G-sharp?

Example 3.24 Gigue, bar 44

A N S W E R 3: G-natural. Notice a similar occurrence in measure 46, where the encircled C is a natural as well (ex. 3.25).

Example 3.25. Gigue, bar 46

Q U E S T I O N 4: In both the above cases, the two notes leading to the trill are preceded by rests. Could this suggest double-dotting, with the two notes in question being foreshortened to sound like a typical trill prefix?

A N S W E R 4: Certainly not. Apart from the fact that the chromatic alteration renders the notion of trill prefix unlikely, almost everything you know about the behavior of concurrent voices in triplet motion should discredit any such conjecture.

PARTITA IV

Ouverture

QUESTION 1: Following my usual procedure, I will first ask you to comment on the title "ouverture."

ANSWER 1: The style and form of the French overture were stabilized by Jean-Baptiste Lully, an Italian who lived and worked in France in the latter part of the seventeenth century. Lully's *ouverture* consisted of a stately opening, a quicker middle section, and an ending similar in character to the beginning. As the title suggests, this well-rounded form was used to introduce successions of dances or as a prelude to an opera. The slow outside portions, usually rather massive in sonority, tended to incorporate the dotted rhythms for which the French had long shown a predilection. In the central section, composers eventually adopted the convention of fugal treatment.

Both the formal design and the character of the French overture seem to have been fixed from the early 1660s, when Lully was the unrivaled arbiter of musical tastes in France. Composers abided by the pattern for almost a hundred years afterwards. Bach infused it with his own ingenuity in his four Suites for orchestra. Strictly speaking, the title "ouverture" refers only to the extended introductory movements, but they so overbalance the dance pieces, or *galanteries,* that comprise the remainder of the Suites that the name "ouverture" has come to identify the whole.

In light of this somewhat oversimplified description of Lully's overture, notice how Bach occasionally modifies the traditional design for his own purposes. In the present example, the initial slow section does not return after the central fugal portion. (Variation 16 of the *Goldberg* set, also entitled "Ouverture," similarly deviates from the traditional pattern.) Suites beginning with this type of movement usually omit the allemande that is present in virtually every aggregation of dances. This Ouverture, however, is followed by the most extended allemande in all of Bach's keyboard works.

QUESTION 2: Is it possible to subject the Ouverture to the same experiment we attempted in the Sinfonia of Partita II, namely, to envision a pulse and retain it throughout?

ANSWER 2: A persistent pulse may help clarify proportions, contrasts, and dramatic effects in this movement. Among other things, you will notice that the tempo or inner activity of the beginning, pervaded as it is with crisply dotted motion, tends to preclude headlong speed. In the 9/8 section you will find controlling forces in the sheer variety of figurations and musical shapes, which follow one another like actors on a stage. Should you run them by too quickly, their individual identities will be undermined. The most obvious of these "actors" is the three-note figure that Bach treats fugally (ex. 4.1):

Example 4.1. Ouverture, bar 18

Another character enters at bar 33 (ex. 4.2):

Example 4.2. Ouverture, bars 33–36

and so on. There are many such controlling factors, of course. Notice the right-hand syncopations in bar 41, the expressive appoggiatura motion in the first two right-hand notes of bars 42 and 43, and the effect of the perfectly measured rests between the quarter notes in the left hand (ex. 4.3).

Example 4.3. Ouverture, bars 41–43

QUESTION 3: I imagine no one disputes that double-dotting is called for in bars 1 to 18.

ANSWER 3: Adherents of double-dotting claim that movements such as this are its native habitat, and editors lend support by aligning notes of unequal value, usually with strong support from the various sources. In bar 5 (ex. 4.4), for example, the final right-hand eighth note is directly aligned with the last sixteenth in the left-hand part, indicating that the two notes are to be struck simultaneously.

Example 4.4. Ouverture, bar 5

This notation occurs so frequently and the double-dotting solution makes such good common sense that even the adversaries of over-dotting have come to accept it.

QUESTION 4: What of double-dotting in the 9/8 section?

ANSWER 4: It stands to reason that the underlying triplet motion takes precedence over all considerations of double-dotting. Any doubts about measure 32, for example, should be dispelled by the virtually identical final bars of the movement, where Bach clarifies his intentions (ex. 4.5).

Example 4.5. Ouverture, bars 111–12

QUESTION 5: I would welcome your guidance regarding the length of the appoggiaturas on the first beats of measures 2 and 5.

ANSWER 5: Whatever you decide, I think it should apply to both bars. I admit to some fondness for an eighth-note duration, not because the appoggiaturas are so written, but because the other musical gestures in this section are so angular that it feels pleasant to hear a sequence of four consecutive, even eighth notes in the upper voice at measure 5 (see example 4.4).

QUESTION 6: What of the left-hand trill between the dotted-eighth-note F-sharp and the sixteenth-note E in bar 6 (ex. 4.6)? The trill symbol seems to be hanging in mid-air.

Example 4.6. Ouverture, bar 6

ANSWER 6: The sources show the trill *between* the notes, as do Henle 1952 and 1979. Bischoff places the symbol squarely above the F-sharp, to the strains of an unenlightening annotation: "These embellishments are misplaced in the sources."* The old Bachgesellschaft edition mindlessly moves

---

*J. S. Bach, *Six Partitas and Overture in French Style,* ed. Hans Bischoff (1882; reprint, New York, 1942), 42*n*2.

the trill onto the low E, without comment. The solution probably lies in play-ing a trill on the F-sharp.

According to Bischoff, the trill symbol on the second quarter-beat of bar 7, right hand, is also "misplaced," although it is difficult to imagine executing the trill anywhere but on the D. Similarly, the mordent symbol between the C-sharp and D in bar 8 clearly applies to the first note. It is wise to remember that certain ornament symbols, such as trills and mordents, typically apply only to specific notes, while others, such as turns, are also used to decorate transitions between notes.* In such cases, there is nothing perplexing about seeing the ornament symbol hanging "in mid-air."

Q U E S T I O N 7: In bar 16 (ex. 4.7) I am perfectly satisfied to play another eighth-note appoggiatura in the left hand. Since this is exactly the value that Bach gives, I am beginning to suspect that it is utter nonsense to suggest that the duration of these "small" notes is unrelated to their written value. The orthographic prescriptions seem to work every time.

Example 4.7. Ouverture, bar 16

A N S W E R 7: Not so fast. Follow me into the 9/8 section. Observe that the appoggiatura in bar 36 is an eighth note, while the small note in bar 40 is a sixteenth (ex. 4.8). If you took these written values literally, could you really defend such a disparity in the context of an obviously sequential design?

Q U E S T I O N 8: Since I presume you are going to say the same thing about the appoggiatura in bar 53, I will proceed to a different matter—the position of the written trill terminations in bars 33 and 37. Should these align with the last note of the left-hand triplet, or should they be dashed off after the third triplet has sounded?

*See the author's *The Harpsichord: A Dialogue for Beginners* (Hackensack, N.J., 1982).

Example 4.8. Ouverture, bars 35–36 and 39–40

ANSWER 8: At bar 33 the two-sixteenth-note termination is perfectly aligned with the third note of the left-hand triplet in the sources, in Henle 1952 and 1979, in the Bachgesellschaft edition, and in Bischoff. In bar 37, however, both Henle editions and the Bachgesellschaft print the termination after the final triplet, apparently to make the sixteenths more legible. (Bischoff, incidentally, bypasses the dilemma by transferring the triplets to the left hand, a practical and wholly innocent departure from the original text.) In performance, the trill termination will be clearer if it coincides with the third note of the left-hand triplet.

Allemande

QUESTION 1: The sheer length of this Allemande is staggering.

ANSWER 1: I would rather have had you say "length and breadth." You will rarely see a movement whose narrative character is so imperturbable. It seems to curl around itself with self-reflections and reminiscences. The solo upper line, while appearing disjointed and improvisatory, is actually iron-clad in its organization.

QUESTION 2: What is a normal length for allemandes? Do their choreographic origins offer any clues, or is there at least an accepted tradition?

ANSWER 2: None that can really be trusted, as you may confirm by looking through the works of Handel, Purcell, the Couperins and others of the French school, Buxtehude, Telemann, Mattheson, Froberger, J. F. K. Fischer, Kuhnau, and so on. This Allemande contains 56 measures. On turning back a few pages you will discover that the Allemande of Partita I has 38 measures, that of Partita II has 32, and that of Partita III a mere 16. Later you will find that the Allemande of Partita V is 28 measures long and that of Partita VI an even 20. So much for any standard of length.

A N S W E R 3: Given the widely varying tempi and characters of Bach's allemandes, I do not see how a pulse can be defined until well after the beginning of each half. The problem is particularly pronounced at bar 25, with its lumbering quarter notes in the left hand. Elsewhere, any pulse quick enough to suggest dance motion threatens to make the graceful figurations and arabesques chatter insipidly. On the other hand, a pulse slow enough to suit the melismatic figurations can be stultifying to both listener and performer. Can you comment?

A N S W E R 3: I suggest you err on the side of slowness. The first opportunity for establishing a pulse is the A–to–D motion in the first measure, left hand (ex. 4.9).

Example 4.9. Allemande, beginning

I think you will find the upbeat note and the first right-hand chord quite powerless to convey a pulse. This does not mean that you should not have a performance speed clearly in mind in advance. It simply means that the A–to–D trajectory is the first time anybody will hear it.

As for bar 25, attempting to impose a ritardando on the preceding measure will greatly increase your risk of throwing the meter wildly out of focus. As much unwinding of momentum as Bach wants at this point has already been written in. My suggestion is to play straight through bar 24 without any fluctuations and keep the eighth-note motion in mind as you enter bar 25. If you still feel uneasy with the "lumbering quarter notes," mentally subdivide the eighth notes into sixteenths until the actual sixteenth-note activity begins.

QUESTION 4: How should one approach the matter of dotting and double-dotting in this movement?

ANSWER 4: That is a weighty question. A classic invitation to double-dotting is provided by the notation on the second beat of measure 13, right hand (ex. 4.10).

Example 4.10. Allemande, bar 13, right hand

But a small tremor of doubt may well assail you in bars 19 and 20 (ex. 4.11), where the bracketed notes in the extended sequence clearly allude to the figure cited above.

Example 4.11. Allemande, bars 19–20, right hand

Opponents of double-dotting claim that rhythmic alterations of this nature betray the character of the allemande and make it difficult to synchronize the left and right hands in certain measures. Moreover, if a note of any duration, when tied over from a previous note, is automatically lengthened and the following notes foreshortened, then many of these additional diminutions become senseless. For example, in measure 9 (ex. 4.12) and others of similar configuration, the thirty-second notes probably will not sound significantly different if they are reduced to sixty-fourths, even at the most conservative tempo.

Example 4.12. Allemande, bar 9, right hand

Those who favor a literal reading further argue that the triplets in the melodic line are intended to contrast with sixteenth notes instead of thirty-seconds. Instability in the sixteenth-note units, as illustrated in example 4.13, would undermine the effect of the interloping triplets.

Example 4.13. Allemande, bar 7, right hand, as written

The same, with double-dotting

Finally, opponents of double-dotting observe that wherever the pattern occurs, as in bar 13, the thirty-second notes constitute a turn from below the main note. The turn needs to be written out because there is no symbol for it in Bach's ornament table, and even if there were, it would suggest that the turn should be played on the beat instead of before the main note.

QUESTION 5: I am certain you will claim that the left hand in this Allemande fulfills nothing more than a basic continuo function. But I find it perplexing that two continuo cellists are operating instead of one. The basic problem seems to lie in hearing and playing two independent continuo voices.

ANSWER 5: The simple harmony causes the two voices to merge like the ingredients in a well-prepared but rather bland stew. The ear will not separate them without the aid of the performer, as we had occasion to observe in the Praeludium of Partita I. A slight emphasis on the left-hand A in bar 1 will not only define the pulse but also help establish the independence of the continuo voices. The problem is not confined to situations of harmonic circumscription. Two-voice textures that move stepwise run an equally great danger of sounding like mere scales if played inattentively. For example, passages like this one in the Ouverture (ex. 4.14)

Example 4.14. Ouverture, bar 25, right hand

run the risk of sounding:

QUESTION 6: Changing the subject, I would like you to traverse the gamut of ornaments in this movement. This should not take long since there appear to be very few.

ANSWER 6: In fact, the ornaments are not so few. Practically the entire right-hand part consists of melismatic elaborations. If, however, you are referring only to ornaments represented by symbols, several are worthy of comment. Please confine your attention to the right hand.

1. Bar 4, second beat: a tied trill.
2. Bar 28, second beat (ex. 4.15): an unusual situation. I think that a *port-de-voix pincé* could easily be the intention here. The customary on-the-beat anticipatory note is not repeated because it is encompassed in the tie.

Example 4.15. Allemande, bar 28, possible realization of *port-de-voix*

An additional complication appears when a trill is imposed on the E on the first beat of bar 28. Although a trill need not necessarily destroy the port-de-voix effect on the F-sharp, particularly at a moderate speed, I regard it as expendable. For one thing, such a rapid succession of ornaments seems excessive. For another, a trill beginning from the F-sharp would undermine both the dissonance created with the D in the left hand and the upward-moving appoggiatura function of the E itself. The effect of reiterating the F-sharp so often would seem mindless anywhere outside the consciously ornate French clavecinists school.

3. Bar 28, second half of third beat: a trill on the thirty-second-note F-sharp. The same ornament occurs on the second half of the first beat of bar 29. Ordinary trills, agreed? Now look back to our discussion of the Sarabande of Partita I (Question and Answer 3) and ahead to bars 13 and 14 of the Sarabande of Partita VI. All self-respecting "thematic interrelators" should add these three passages to their compendium of irrelevancies.

4. Bar 30, third note: an ordinary mordent.

5. Bar 39, last beat: a tied trill.

Courante

QUESTION 1: It seems clear that the small-note appoggiaturas cannot possibly all be of equal duration, particularly given their abundance throughout the piece. Am I right?

ANSWER 1: There is nothing to fear from the first of these small notes, in bar 4 (ex. 4.16), which merely indicates a slightly lengthened upper note for the trill initiation.

Example 4.16. Courante, bar 4

The first possible troublemaker is the appoggiatura before the G-natural on the fourth beat of the same measure. If your interpretation of the natural motion of the piece leads you to prefer an eighth-note duration, you will plunge headlong into parallel fifths with the bass voice. Should this cause you smolderings of conscience, then by all means play the appoggiatura as a sixteenth note, although this alternative may seem charmless in later measures. Wait and see how you feel after penetrating more deeply into the movement. Do not fail to take into account bar 8 (ex. 4.17), where the appoggiatura function is written in full-value notes.

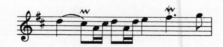

Example 4.17. Courante, bar 8, right hand

QUESTION 2: In measure 6, most modern editions show C-sharp at the point marked by the arrow in example 4.18.

Example 4.18. Courante, bar 6, right hand

Bars 1, 3, and 4 in the right hand and bar 2 in the left have accustomed the ear to the melodic interval of a fourth at that position in the motif. What do the sources say?

A N S W E R 2 : I agree that the note probably should be B-natural. The majority of sources, however, say C-sharp. Henle 1979, which gives B-natural, cites the copy of the 1731 edition at the University of Illinois as the source for the correction.

Q U E S T I O N 3 : At bar 15 (ex. 4.19), there is a slur on the fifth and sixth beats in the right hand. Does this simply indicate a tied trill? It seems to embrace too many notes.

Example 4.19. Courante, bar 15, right hand

A N S W E R 3 : Not only does the slur take in too many notes to be an exact instruction for a tied trill, it also has no equivalent at bar 39, which is a virtually identical cadential situation. Furthermore, if a tied trill were the answer, the two sixteenth notes following the B-natural might be rhythmically weakened, particularly at an animated courante pulse. It has been suggested that the rhythmic and melodic demands made on the two sixteenths are well beyond those required of mere trill terminations. It is possible that the slur is a slip of the pen, but if so, it is a mighty slip, as the slur appears in all sources.

Q U E S T I O N 4 : May I presume that the written value of the appoggiaturas on beats 1 and 5 of bar 32 need not concern me?

A N S W E R 4 : Peace be upon you, dear friend! No one has ever said that the notation of small notes need not concern you. It has merely been observed that the written values do not always translate literally into sound. In this case, however, the orthography seems correct. As an example of the contrary, compare the sixteenth-note appoggiatura at bar 38 to bar 14, where the same ornamental note is written as an eighth note (ex. 4.20).

Example 4.20. Courante, bars 38 and 14, right hand

QUESTION 5: What is the verdict on double-dotting in this Courante?

ANSWER 5: If you can find situations in which double-dotting is justified by the notation, does not weaken the highly assertive rhythmic motifs, and does not result in hysterical foreshortening of already extremely short notes—then do it! If you cannot fulfill these requirements, then, once again, be careful of what you read in books.

Aria

QUESTION 1: Is it not unusual for such a movement to be interposed before the Sarabande? Miscellaneous pieces are normally relegated to a position after the traditional allemande–courante–sarabande sequence.

ANSWER 1: There is only one other instance in the Partitas of such an "accessory" movement preceding the sarabande, in Partita VI. That movement is entitled "Air," not Aria, and was obviously added for the 1731 compilation, there being no trace of it in the earlier version of the partita in the *Notebook* of Anna Magdalena.

In the "Overture in the French Manner" (part 2 of the *Clavier-Übung*), you will find Gavottes I and II and Passepieds I and II inserted before the Sarabande, but such intrusions do not occur elsewhere in Bach's three major keyboard suite-groups. There are movements entitled "Air" in French Suites II and IV, but they appear after the Sarabandes.

QUESTION 2: My next question has several parts:

1. Can this Aria have been an afterthought, as you suggest the Air was in Partita VI?

2. Can it have been motivated solely by a desire to have seven movements in each partita?

3. Could the Aria have been placed before the Sarabande to achieve a sharper contrast between movements?

ANSWER 2: One may well ask how many afterthoughts Bach was prepared to allow himself in a single partita. It would seem that he consumed his quota in the Menuet, whose messy appearance is all the more striking in that the presentation of the Partitas is otherwise pristine.

It is inconclusive to suggest that Bach wanted each partita to have seven movements. In any case, the number of movements would not explain the position of the Aria before the Sarabande. As for the element of contrast, I think you will agree that this would be provided by a transition from the Courante directly into the Sarabande (as we will also find in Partita VI).

QUESTION 3: What can you say about the title? I find very little of the lyrical or songlike here.

ANSWER 3: Although the term *aria* implies a voice-related musical entity, it can encompass broader areas of expression than those to which we traditionally confine it. In this case, the music is earthy, even somewhat raucous, evoking a certain peasant joviality. Perhaps we should try to think of Papa Bach holding a stein of beer in his hand and bellowing some rustic tune in the company of his family and friends. Should you find the usual connotations of the title "aria" impossible to lay aside, try taking the stein out of Bach's hand and replacing it with a Bible; try forcing him to be lyrical and poetic while the bass is stamping out the strong beats under the syncopated right-hand melody in the first eight bars; or try playing such passages as bars 40 to 45 (ex. 4.21) with a cantabile approach.

Example 4.21. Aria, bars 40–45

Perhaps more important than all this is the fact that the Aria, its title not-withstanding, exploits the keyboard as unabashedly as any of Bach's music. For example, compare the two statements of the melody in the opening bars (ex. 4.22).

Example 4.22. Aria, bars 1–7

This is keyboard idiom and even something beyond; Bach is using the key-board instrument as a miniature orchestra. Notice the "reorchestration" of the accompaniment: the blatant clangor in bars 4 to 7 contrasts with the forthright but not nearly so resonant initial delivery in bars 1 to 4. This is an age-old harpsichord device. The instrument itself will not permit the second statement of the melody to sound otherwise than as a confirmation made many times more powerful by increased textural density. Try to remember this the next time you hear a pianist play an "echo" here merely because it is the second appearance of a melodic event.

Were I to compile a catalogue of sound effects that are idiomatic to the keyboard or that use it to transcribe other instrumental sonorities, I would certainly mention bars 41 and 43 (example 4.21). I would also single out bar 45, where the abrupt interruption of the running motion, followed by the diminution of the right-hand F-sharp to a sixteenth note, produces a startling instrumental sound, as if Bach thought the train was running too smoothly and needed to be momentarily derailed! When the F-sharp triad blasts into the texture in the left hand, we have an instrumental detonation worthy of Domenico Scarlatti himself. Beware of any keyboard teacher who asks you to roll this chord or soften its impact to any degree. What purpose other than sheer shock would such a thick chord, particularly one surrounded by gasping eighth-note rests, have in such a low range of the keyboard?

Q U E S T I O N 4: From about bar 46 to the end, do I see another of those organic crescendi we have spoken of before?

A N S W E R 4: You do indeed. The music is being propelled forward and upward, but be careful of accelerating. Try thinking of the apparent intensification of sound as merely something that happens, not something you do. Your task is to feel the propulsion and follow it, paradoxically without deliberate velocity changes in either direction. Chances are that an accelerando feeling will appear by itself.

Q U E S T I O N 5: Is it not curious that Bach uses the Italian word *aria* in a partita that begins with a French overture, and the French word *air* in Partita VI, which begins with a movement bearing the Italian title "Toccata"?

A N S W E R 5: Now that you mention it, I suppose it is curious, but it does not seem incongruous with Bach's general esthetic approach. He sometimes makes a point of separating the French and Italian styles, as in part 2 of the *Clavier-Übung*, which contains both a "Concerto in the Italian Taste" and an "Overture in the French Manner." At other times Bach's art represents history's most perfect synthesis of the two styles. The efforts of musicologists to isolate the French and Italian influences that Bach so thoughtfully amalgamated are primarily interesting studies in abstract historical curiosity.

Sarabande

QUESTION 1: Although this movement looks a little harrowing on the printed page, my initial attempts to play it have somehow endeared it to me. For one thing, it seems to belong exactly where it is. I could not envision it as a member of any other suite arrangement but this one.

ANSWER 1: I am delighted that your running quarrel with sarabandes is finally becoming more well-tempered. After all, the variety and ingenuity of these movements is a treasure, not an invitation to bewilderment. Glance very quickly at a half page or so of the preceding Allemande and then do the same with the Sarabande. The superficial similarity of appearance between the two movements is hardly a matter of musical significance, but it tends to support your intuition that the Sarabande belongs exactly where it is.

QUESTION 2: This very feature filled me with apprehension at first. However, I soon discovered that the Sarabande is, in many ways, extraordinarily compact, well controlled by obvious "continuo" motion in the left hand, and generously endowed with sequences and other joints and sutures that hold it together in performance. In this connection, dare I interpret measure 29 as a recapitulation?

ANSWER 2: It is quite common in the second half of a binary piece to repeat a thematic gesture that occurs in the first half. By Bach's time, the binary form was rarely the monolithic prison cell we are told about in music appreciation classes. Composers had infused it with remarkable flexibility, often using a feeling of recapitulation to compensate for the rigidity of the form. Countless sonatas by Domenico Scarlatti, for example, show a type of "development" technique in the second half that makes one wonder whether it is wise to execute repeats according to the formerly sacrosanct requirements of the binary design.

QUESTION 3: Have you any comment on the ties in example 4.23?

Example 4.23. Sarabande, bar 19, right hand

These appear neither in the Bachgesellschaft edition nor in Bischoff. I have found them only in Henle 1979, where they are surrounded by parentheses.

A N S W E R 3: I would reject the ties, if I were you. In addition to being omitted from a number of modern editions, they are not well supported in the sources. Take care, however, not to apply the same advice to bar 33. Here the ties are legitimate. The entire measure hovers harmonically before being unleashed at bar 34. The ties contribute to that effect.

Q U E S T I O N 4: In measure 14 (ex. 4.24), does the number "6" above the sixteenth notes appear in the earliest sources? After some of the archaic conventions of notation we have encountered, the spectacle of a "sexolet" (I believe that is the correct word) seems unexpectedly modern.

Example 4.24. Sarabande, bar 14

A N S W E R 4: The number "6" is indeed in the originals and means exactly what it would in music of more recent vintage.

Q U E S T I O N 5: The small-note appoggiatura at bar 20 is written as a sixteenth. Can one abide by that?

A N S W E R 5: Yes again. It may be helpful to relate it in your ear to the first and last beats of measure 28 (ex. 4.25).

Example 4.25. Sarabande, bars 20 and 28, right hand

Menuet

QUESTION 1: Could the written-out turn in bar 1 (ex. 4.26) have been represented by the symbol ∽ ?

Example 4.26. Menuet, bar 1, right hand

ANSWER 1: The turn symbol indicates the configuration of the ornament, but does not fully prescribe its metrical position. Notice that the symbol is used again on the last beat of bar 19. This means that the turn is to be played on the beat, not before, and is not affected by dotted motion or subject to the demands of triplets. The turn merely decorates the leading-tone function of the A-sharp moving across the bar line to the key of B minor.

QUESTION 2: There is an unmistakable dot over the G on the third beat of measure 1. Is this in the original?

ANSWER 2: The dot is in all the sources. It appears on the third beats of measures 1 and 5, but not in bars 21 and 25, where consistency might lead you to expect it. The dot may easily connote a staccato articulation, but for a fuller discussion of its significance, please reread Question and Answer 2 in the section on the Burlesca of Partita III.

QUESTION 3: What sort of dangerous rhythmic collision is taking place between the outer voices at bar 14 (ex. 4.27)?

Example 4.27. Menuet, bar 14

ANSWER 3: Either try two-against-three (which may be frowned upon by those who insist that triplets must have their own way) or double-dot the F-sharp on the first beat, left hand, so that the rhythm becomes ♩. ♫♪ ♪.

QUESTION 4: Can that be a slur over the left hand at bar 22 (ex. 4.28)?

Example 4.28. Menuet, bar 22

ANSWER 4: Yes, and it appears in all the sources. View it as a phrasing suggestion, as a demand for legato which you would have granted anyway (since there are few alternatives), or as a birthday greeting from your Aunt Gertrude. But play it just as it is written!

Gigue

QUESTION 1: You have occasionally stressed the need to be aware of the difference between note-groups that outline simple harmonies and other groups that move the ear from note to note. Your point seemed to be that the player's technical approach might somehow be conditioned by such insights. What, then, is expected of a player faced with a fairly fast-moving gigue in fugal style, the subject of which opens with a D major arpeggio? Can any keyboard player arouse interest in the subject of a fugue, fulfill the simultaneous requirements of harmonic and melodic delivery, and dance a gigue, all at the same time?

ANSWER 1: This may be a case of embarrassment of riches rather than of ambiguity, as your question implies. Consider the following suggestions:

1. A gigue should be played at an appropriate tempo. This does not mean a speed at which a resident orthopedist is required "just in case." Nevertheless, it will not be slow.

2. Observance of exact note values must be assumed.

3. A well-chosen pulse will allow for a slight staccato executed by the fin-

gers, not by the hand or any other such unwieldy mechanism. Such minute detachments may well contribute to the desired "gigueness."

4. No incisive upbeat note issues in the subject, as in the Gigue of Partita III. Instead you have a long first note that is quite powerless by itself. The following short note (F-sharp) must, therefore, be relied on to generate motion.

5. The high D at the top of the ascending arpeggio in bar 1 may be attacked resolutely, thus enhancing the contrast with the C-natural in bar 2, in spite of the hammering downbeats that may result.

6. Once the aforesaid C-natural sounds, you are in business. This note threatens the stability of the D major tonality and creates a harmonic question mark, so to speak. The fugue subject then punctuates itself jauntily and with a kind of mischievous cleverness. In fact, the embarrassment of riches I mentioned lies largely in the fact that even if you play the Gigue quite badly—that is, with either excessive legato or a hysterically pointillistic touch—the music is likely to dance for you all the same.

QUESTION 2: What is this squirming for six measures at the start of the second half (ex. 4.29)? Surely one is not expected to regard this as an inversion of the opening subject.

Example 4.29. Gigue, bars 49–54

ANSWER 2: Not exactly, to be sure. This passage may be looked upon as a new subject, since Bach amply treats it as such. You may also view it as a countersubject to the principal theme of the first half, since it often behaves that way as well. However you choose to define it, you may simply go on with your triplet cantering for as long as the material allows. The original fugue subject will soon reappear like a cavalry regiment to the rescue. A clear example of this occurs at bar 55 (ex. 4.30), where the two subjects coincide perfectly.

Example 4.30. Gigue, bar 55

Q U E S T I O N 3: I am somewhat taken aback by the shameless, Donizetti-like oom-pah-pah accompaniment at measures 29 to 32 (ex. 4.31).

Example 4.31. Gigue, bars 29–32

A N S W E R 3: Other incidents of similar boisterousness occur elsewhere in this partita—for example, at bars 41 to 43 in the Ouverture. Bach also exploits the device outrageously at bars 41 to 44 of the Aria, where the rhythm is oom-pah-pah-pah.

PARTITA V

Praeambulum

QUESTION 1: Would it be too obvious to suggest that Bach used the title "praeambulum" here because a "praeludium" already existed in Partita I?

ANSWER 1: Your guess is probably as good as any. It is interesting to compare the Latin roots of *praeludium* and *praeambulum*. The common prefix *prae* suggests something that comes before. The Latin word *ludus* means a game or diversion. *Ambulum,* on the other hand, derives from *ambulare,* roughly meaning to wander or even to go astray. The fact that the Praeludium in Partita I is only twenty-one measures long, whereas the present Praeambulum contains ninety-five bars, may give birth to the idea that all movements entitled "praeambulum" are very extended. Be careful of such nonsense. The individual pieces comprising the Sinfonias, or Three-Part Inventions, were originally entitled "praeambulum," although they are neither conspicuously long nor given to wandering.

QUESTION 2: Actually, I hear both the Sinfonia of Partita II and the Ouverture of Partita IV as much longer works than this Praeambulum.

ANSWER 2: Perhaps so, but there are those who would disagree with you on the grounds that both the Sinfonia and the Ouverture are clearly subdivided internally. The Praeambulum, by contrast, has only two frontiers: its beginning and its end.

QUESTION 3: The first four measures (ex. 5.1) seem charged with a shock element that one finds difficult to associate with almighty and always self-controlled Bach. Can you comment?

Example 5.1. Praeambulum, bars 1–4

ANSWER 3: Surely you have heard Bach "kick open the front door" before: the beginnings of some of his most portentous organ works burst into the air like claps of thunder. Notice that these four bars recur periodically in different keys as a unifying element in the Praeambulum, almost as if Bach were testing the potentialities of some uninhibited rondo pattern. Notice, too, that the four bars divide themselves in the middle, as if the first two were to be understood as a grammatical "subject" and the second two as a "predicate."

QUESTION 4: The notation of this passage seems to leave little doubt that the chords call for a rather pugnacious attack.

ANSWER 4: You are right in principle, but the observation is incomplete. Notice, for example, the built-in dynamic difference between the chords in bar 4 and those in bars 1 and 2. The chords in bar 4 are not only heavier, they also reach further into the ponderous bass range of the keyboard. You will observe these same characteristics in all reappearances of this four-bar statement. This is organic dynamics at its most obvious, although it is easily overlooked by less perceptive performers.

Another matter to be considered is the effect of the rests, which are as important as the notes themselves. The releases of the chords must be absolutely exact, as if the sound had been electrically deactivated, or the impact of the passage will be diminished. This is intended as a warning for pianists in particular, not only because the fatter tone of their instrument is apt to intrude upon the rests, but because their traditional concern with "singing tone" and other irrelevancies tends to make them discount the importance of an abrupt cessation of sound. Another obvious peril lies in excessive speed. It would be absurd to deny that this Praeambulum demands considerable virtuoso flair, but this is not a matter of mere haste. You may find the rests a good guide in this regard. If, for example, you cannot hear dead silence between the chords in bars 1 through 4, you are very likely to be playing too fast.

QUESTION 5: I am bothered by the naked scales in bars 5, 6, and 7. Although they are not as difficult as some, the different keyboard configurations can cause unevenness of sound not only within a given scale, but between one scale and the next.

ANSWER 5: You are probably striving for evenness by the purely gymnastic process of playing evenly. You had that problem in the Allemande of Partita I, when you attempted to play the arpeggiated figurations relying exclusively on mechanics. How ironic that the very evenness of tone that piano-oriented musicians often deride as one of the harpsichord's acoustical shortcomings can be the effect they find most difficult to attain! To be sure, the Praeambulum presents a problem that did not exist in Partita I: playing scales may lead you to adhere so strictly to the fingering orthodoxies of the "rotation system," inculcated in all modern players, that you do not feel free to experiment properly with phrase shapes and note groupings. If so, set aside the rotation system momentarily and see what comes about. You may even wish to redistribute the notes between the hands. Do not, however, forgo a slight lengthening of the first note of each rising scale. Particularly on the harpsi-

Example 5.2. Praeambulum, bars 8–14

chord, you will need these notes to keep the ear informed of what is happening harmonically.

QUESTION 6: What say you about the figurations in bars 8 to 14 (ex. 5.2)?

ANSWER 6: For both technical and musical reasons, a distinction of touch should again be made between arpeggios and notes that move stepwise. The latter should be played more crisply and without the overlapping sonorities that are appropriate in arpeggiated passages, where the objective is to delineate harmonic fields. Clearly articulating the stepwise motion is all the more desirable because the bracketed notes in example 5.2 provide a strong upbeat to help the player across the bar line.

QUESTION 7: In the Bischoff edition, the marking "MD" is applied to the bottom note of the arpeggios in bars 8, 10, 12, and 14. This can only mean that the right hand is to cross over (or under) the left. Does this marking appear in the sources? I have attempted following this instruction and find it very practical indeed.

ANSWER 7: The sources, of course, contain no such marking. The notes in question are merely stemmed upward and beamed separately. Since the orthography throughout this movement betrays some preoccupation with the distribution of notes between hands, however, Bischoff has proposed a few solutions of his own. When a knowledgeable editor takes such initiatives, they are often worth serious consideration. In this case, Bischoff's "MD" indication can be seen as a technical practicality, rather than as an infringement on the purity of the original text.

QUESTION 8: Measures 8 to 14, like 1 to 4, seem to dovetail by pairs.

ANSWER 8: You are right. Tension at bar 8 gives way to comparative relaxation at bar 9, and so on. Furthermore, each measure is connected to the next by stepwise melodic motion until the sequential procedure breaks at bar 15.

QUESTION 9: The unchanging continuo motion of the left hand at bars 21 to 24 (ex. 5.3) seems very welcome after all the stopping and starting of the previous measures.

Example 5.3. Praeambulum, bars 21–24

ANSWER 9: Quite so, but do not underestimate the significance of that bass merely because it is written in eighth notes. That it can be considered a little more important than a mere continuo pattern will become clear to you if you examine bars 69 to 71, where the same eight-note figure appears in a conspicuously thematic guise (ex. 5.4).

Example 5.4. Praeambulum, bars 69–71

This confirms the wisdom of what I am sure you have been doing all along—initiating your phrase motion from the second of these eighth notes, not from the first.

QUESTION 10: Do you recommend a ritardando leading into the fermata at bar 86?

ANSWER 10: Do not flirt with danger. A broadening of tempo is already taking place because of the increasingly wide intervals and mounting dissonance in the left hand. Slowing down too much might render the right hand completely unmanageable. Perhaps you could pull back slightly on the last two eighth-note beats of measure 85, holding the fermata only as long as will enable you to maintain tension. Remember that suspense, if overextended, will simply dissipate. This is no time for seductive subtleties of sound.

Allemande

QUESTION 1: There is nothing uncommon about a 4/4 time signature in an allemande, but do the wall-to-wall triplets in this movement forecast problems?

ANSWER 1: Yes, there could be trouble afoot. A controversial figuration arises on the very first right-hand beat of measure 1 (ex. 5.5).

Example 5.5. Allemande, bar 1, right hand, as written

Innocent as the two thirty-second notes may appear, there is sharp disagreement over their interpretation. Members of the "assimilation" school argue that all motion concurrent with triplets, or even taking place in a context in which triplets predominate, must be assimilated rhythmically into that triplet motion. In their view, the thirty-second notes should be played as in example 5.6:

Example 5.6. Allemande, bar 1, right hand, with triplet rhythm

Nonassimilators hold that the thirty-second notes are answerable to an even more commanding call, one clearly suggested in bar 12 and irrefutably confirmed in bar 28 (ex. 5.7).

The thirty-second notes in bar 12 seem to be a deliberate recollection of bar 1 in its literal, nonassimilated form. Opponents of assimilation argue that a single notation of this sort could well be mistaken for some sort of orthographic shorthand, but its repetition at bars 12, 13, and 28 suggests that Bach intended it to be interpreted as an unalterable rhythmic gesture. They point

Example 5.7. Allemande, bars 12 and 28

out that this notational device is not explicable in terms of Bach's usual writing habits, unless he meant it to be played literally.

I confess to harboring some sympathy for both points of view. I am impressed by the inflexible conviction of the assimilation school, but my interest is also aroused by the nonassimilators' contention that the subject of triplets cannot be viewed panoramically. In view of the many perplexing incidents in Bach's music, I am inclined to believe that it is safer to do without a general rule than to adopt one that merely draws attention to the exceptions.

Q U E S T I O N 2: If I were to take your words to heart, every measure in this movement would prompt questions regarding triplets and the material surrounding them!

A N S W E R 2: Look more closely. Your impression is not correct. I do not see any incident—with the possible exception of the end of bar 20, which we will discuss in a moment—that cannot be deciphered by applying information already in your possession. The apparent difficulties in measure 4 (ex. 5.8), for example, can be overcome simply by remembering certain facts. The slur encompassing the two right-hand sixteenth notes on the second beat does not merely indicate legato; it confirms the appoggiatura function of the B-natural. Relax. You almost certainly would not have detached the two notes anyway—that is, unless you did not wish to live to play measure 5.

Example 5.8. Allemande, bar 4

Measure 17 (ex. 5.9) should cause you no perplexity at all. This is truly assimilation with a will. The solution is quite elementary: it should be played as written.

Example 5.9. Allemande, bar 17

As to the second half of measure 20 (ex. 5.10), the matter is not so simple. There seems to be a bona fide choice between playing the two-against-three pattern as written or imposing a type of *notes inégales* motion in the left hand, in accordance with the assimilation doctrine.

Example 5.10. Allemande, bar 20, as written

The same, with left-hand rhythm adjusted

QUESTION 3: I see no serious problems with ornaments in this movement. Am I overlooking something?

ANSWER 3: No problems, but a few minor nuisances in the first three measures. Many editions print a mordent on the last note in the right hand of bar 1. This is patently absurd. The mordent belongs on the D immediately preceding. On the fourth beat of measure 2, the right-hand appoggiatura should probably be a sixteenth note, as written. However graceful an eighth note may seem, it would produce an undesirable parallel octave with the left-hand triplets. There is little melodic necessity for giving the appoggiaturas in bars 2 and 3 the same value (ex. 5.11). If you feel that a left-hand sixteenth note in bar 3 would sound unpleasantly abrupt against the flowing triplets in the right hand, you must simply lengthen the appoggiatura to an eighth note and sacrifice consistency.

Example 5.11. Allemande, bars 2–3

Corrente

QUESTION 1: I am in favor of a quicker pulse here than in any corrente we have examined thus far. Is this correct?

ANSWER 1: Probably so. In the Corrente of Partita I you must account for the clarity of triplet shapes; the Courante of Partita II is of the French type, with all the attendant complexities of its species. The Corrente of Partita III, although not devoid of forward-driving momentum, is punctuated by an unyielding dotted motion that loses its profile beyond a certain speed, and the Courante of Partita IV again abides by the more deliberate French standards of tempo.

In this movement the road seems to have been cleared of almost every obstacle. It is paved with typical keyboard figuration, the harmonic picture is quite simple for the most part, the metrical unit is seductively uniform, and the left-hand "continuo player" seems quite happy with his lot (at least through the first half of the movement). In any case, Italian correntes are not expected to be slow. I would only caution you against playing so fast that you obscure the flirtatious rhythmic displacements in the first four left-hand measures and in bars 5, 6, and 7 in the right hand. Should you do so, you may cross the line between a burst of virtuoso exuberance and a commonplace finger exercise.

Q U E S T I O N 2: May we discuss the large dots above the last two right-hand notes of measure 23 (ex. 5.12)? I recall that a similar notation occurred in the Burlesca of Partita III and in the Menuet of Partita IV. It seemed to me that we did not do very well with them then, and I wonder if we can arrive at a more enlightening explanation here.

Example 5.12. Corrente, bar 23, right hand

A N S W E R 2: The dot over the F-sharp clearly indicates staccato. In the case of the E, you will have noticed that both a Trillo und Mordant symbol and a dot surmount it. The idea seems to be that the ornament should not be allowed to merge into the D that begins the next measure. In other words, the ornament is to be isolated from what would normally be considered its note of resolution. I advise you to reread our discussion of the Trillo und Mordant in the Sarabande of Partita III.

An almost inevitable result of these detachments will be a slight break in speed at this point. This will be particularly noticeable if you have chosen to play this Corrente very fast. Within reason, I would not let this worry you. The momentary arrest of the chatter of running notes is probably intentional, given that the dots are placed over two eighth notes.

Q U E S T I O N 3: Speaking of "chatter," the music seems to run headlong into an unopened door in the cadences at bars 31–32 and 63–64 (ex. 5.13). What about making ritards at those points?

Example 5.13. Corrente, bars 31–32 and 63–64

A N S W E R 3: I would reserve your ritardando for the very end of the piece, and apply only a very slight one even then. Bach has again built in a pulling back of the reins, as indicated by the augmentation of note values, the opening of the two-part texture to three voices, and, particularly in measures 63 and 64, the plunging of the left hand into the depths of the keyboard range.

Q U E S T I O N 4: Should the eighth notes in these same bars be detached?

A N S W E R 4: In the right hand perhaps, but absolutely not in the left; the lowness of the tones precludes it. In any case, you must not detach all the parts to the same degree or you will hear nothing.

Sarabande

Q U E S T I O N 1: Having previously expressed some discomfort in slow movements, I hasten to say that I consider this Sarabande a perfect vehicle for the harpsichord. Its sound seems to enhance the music's rather wistful eloquence. No doubt this is due to the abundant decoration that gives the movement its embroidered appearance on the page. On the other hand, this ornamental filigree presents problems for the performer.

A N S W E R 1: Quite so, and you must start your fine-tooth combing of the ornamentation at the upbeat measure. I have a few prescriptions that may serve you well. To begin with, pay close attention to the written values of the small notes, contrary to what is so often recommended. Consider the interpretation of the opening bars (ex. 5.14):

Example 5.14. Sarabande, beginning

Double-dotting has been assumed for the moment, this being the wrong place to dwell on its controversial aspects. Moreover, the very first sixteenth-note minor third (B–D) should be slightly separated from the double appoggiatura in the upbeat bar. Further support for literally observing the written values of the small notes is found in bar 2. On the first beat, notice that the double appoggiatura in the right hand is written in eighth notes, whereas the simultaneous appoggiatura in the left hand is a sixteenth. Why? Because moving both appoggiaturas to their respective notes of resolution in exact synchronization would produce parallel fifths between the outer voices. (There is considerable evidence that Bach thought little of this misdemeanor, but that does not mean he actually sought parallel fifths on any occasion!)

The obvious solution is to follow the small-note written values literally. The sixteenth-note appoggiatura in the left hand must reach its destination (G-sharp) before the right hand moves. Would that I could give you equal confidence in the orthography of every small-note figure that might ever cross your path, but this is not to be had. In measure 18, for example, the appoggiaturas coincide exactly as in measure 2. A copy of the 1731 edition at the University of Illinois depicts the left-hand appoggiatura as an eighth note. This must be an error, as it is not substantiated by any other source. I mention it only because Henle 1979 chose to reprint it, providing what I consider to be an unnecessary perplexity.

QUESTION 2: Your prescriptions do seem to solve most of the problems in this movement, but I notice several exceptions. In particular, a literal execution of the eighth-note appoggiatura in bar 4 seems to destroy the "rhyme" I would have enjoyed at bar 8, where a similar figure is rendered as a quarter note (ex. 5.15).

Example 5.15. Sarabande, bars 4 and 8

ANSWER 2: Perhaps so, and perhaps not. This is a matter of notational orthodoxy. The oncoming event in the left hand of bar 8 may somehow have affected Bach's choice of orthography. This may also be true in bar 4, since the eighth note following the dotted quarter in the right hand would have been reduced to a sixteenth, in accordance with the prevailing rhythmic nucleus of the piece. In any case, if you are determined to produce your "rhyme," you can consider the appoggiatura in bar 4 an exception and lengthen it to your satisfaction.

QUESTION 3: In bar 9 (ex. 5.16), is the final eighth note in the right hand aligned with the sixteenth in the middle voice, as many modern editors would have us believe?

Example 5.16. Sarabande, bar 9, right hand

ANSWER 3: Yes, the notes are so aligned in the sources. You will notice that the eighth-note B follows a dotted quarter and is thereby subject to double-dotting, for those so minded. This would make it a sixteenth note, to be sounded simultaneously with the D in the middle voice.

QUESTION 4: Could you explain the small, hooklike ornament at bars 20 and 22?

ANSWER 4: Examples 5.17 and 5.18 show the basic form of the ornament as deciphered in Bach's own table, and its application in the present context.

ANSWER 2: Yes, provided your ear retains control over the conduct of voices. A technical solution should not create a musical problem, any more than the reverse.

QUESTION 3: I quake with terror at some of the ornaments in store in this movement.

ANSWER 3: Take heart: you are not alone. The second half of the Gigue has undermined the confidence of even the most stalwart keyboard players for more than two centuries. First, let us try to clear the air. The problem arises most clearly at measure 34 in the 1731 edition (ex. 5.23).

Example 5.23. Gigue, bars 34–37

Like other extant sources, this particular "horse's mouth" offers certain hardships. For one thing, the ornament ___ in bar 34 seems to be missing, although by rights the symbol belongs on the second C-sharp of the left hand. In bars 36 and 37 the ornament symbol is much clearer, and it is at this point that trouble begins.

Assuming the symbol to be intended in bar 34, a glance at Bach's table of ornaments will identify it as a Doppelt-Cadence, to be deciphered as

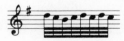

This would mean that the motion B-natural–to–C-sharp will be heard three times: in the written prefix to the trill, in the course of the Doppelt-Cadence

represented by the symbol, and in the written termination. Clearly, a literal realization of the ornament at gigue tempo presents almost superhuman technical difficulties. A practical solution is to regard the prefix indication in the symbol as an invitation to lengthen the upper neighbor of the trill and thereby enhance its appoggiatura function. Since even this will be exceedingly difficult to play in many cases, it is generally considered permissible to play a straightforward trill wherever the ornament appears.

QUESTION 4: How do you explain the diminution of the last righthand E in measure 49 from the expected eighth note to a sixteenth (ex. 5.24)?

Example 5.24. Gigue, bar 49

ANSWER 4: You have doubtless observed that this sixteenth note not only initiates a statement of the subject of the second half of the Gigue, it also introduces an inverted form of the subject of the first half in the uppermost voice. Moreover, the entire second half of bar 49 conforms to the shape of the sixteenth-note portion of the Gigue's subject after the double bar (ex. 5.25).

Example 5.25. Gigue, bar 33, left hand

Perhaps Bach thought enough of the configuration of the bracketed notes to maintain it unaltered. Among the other explanations that have been ventured is the conjecture that the shortened E was intended to provide time for the player to change manuals on the harpsichord. This is an attractive idea, but virtually impossible to support in light of what we know about Bach's habits of notation.

PARTITA VI

Toccata

QUESTION 1: This movement, like the Sinfonia of Partita II, is sometimes said to be a French overture.

ANSWER 1: Again, misunderstandings may arise because the more you press for a definition of "toccata form," the more you alienate yourself from the fundamental freedom that characterizes works so entitled. Suffice it to say that a toccata is a player's piece, one that shows off the instrumentalist's touch and other skills, in contrast to a cantata, which involves singing. These skills are not confined to the gymnastic virtuosities demanded by more recent toccata composers. Bach's harpsichord toccatas test the performer's mettle in everything from recitative to complex fugues, from lyrical introspection to the heights of instrumental brilliance.

QUESTION 2: Would you recommend the "underlying pulse" experiment in this toccata, as you did in the Sinfonia of Partita II and the Ouverture of Partita IV?

ANSWER 2: Emphatically yes. A consistent pulse is especially vital here for two reasons. First, the fugal section of the movement begins in the same measure in which the introductory section ends (ex. 6.1). There is no change of time signature before the initial statement of the subject, as there was in Partitas II and IV.

Example 6.1. Toccata, bars 26–27

Second, important material from the introductory section reappears in bars 71–72, 85–86, and elsewhere in the fugue. These repetitions exert a unifying force that would be impaired if the material were presented at different tempi.

QUESTION 3: In figurations like the one in measure 1 (ex. 6.2), should the notes of the rising arpeggio be held over to accumulate into a full chord?

Example 6.2. Toccata, bar 1

ANSWER 3: Whatever decision you make is sure to be disputed. Those against over-holding the notes claim that there is no explicit notational demand for doing so in either the final 1731 version of the partita or in the earlier *Notebook* of Anna Magdalena Bach. Furthermore, when Bach wanted the arpeggiated notes to be sustained into a chord, he jolly well knew how to write it (ex. 6.3).

Example 6.3. Partita VI, Sarabande, bar 2

Those in favor of over-holding argue that basic musical literacy demands it, particularly given the acoustical properties of keyboard instruments. They point out that Bach lengthened the first note of the arpeggio from a thirty-second note in the Anna Magdalena version to a sixteenth note in the 1731 revision. This strengthened the bass and allowed him to pile something on top of it, as illustrated by Ferruccio Busoni's famous transcription of the partita (ex. 6.4).

Example 6.4. Toccata, bars 1–2, Busoni transcription (© by Breitkopf & Härtel, Wiesbaden)

Q U E S T I O N 4: Are you in favor of literally observing the written values of the arpeggiated notes?

A N S W E R 4: Yes. The fact that Bach changed the note values when he revised the Toccata suggests that he was not entirely indifferent to the matter. Moreover, the arpeggios appear repeatedly in pairs, operate sequentially, and are a nuclear element in the movement. Symmetry would therefore seem to be desirable, and it can best be achieved by playing the notes as written. The more improvisational character of the notation at bar 3 (ex. 6.5) is likely to benefit retroactively from the contrast.

Example 6.5. Toccata, bar 3, right hand

Q U E S T I O N 5: The last time I asked a question about thematic inter-relation, you got the better of me. Nevertheless, you must surely admit that there is a motivic kinship between the beginning of the Toccata (exx. 6.2 and 6.3) and the subject of the fugue (ex. 6.1).

A N S W E R 5: I admit it and rejoice in it! This descending second is the so-called sigh motive that appears occasionally in Bach's works. It often produces problems in voice leading, particularly when a trill appears on the first note. Some players avert these problems by interpreting the trill symbol as a "short trill" (a three-note ornament starting from the main note), an inverted mordent, or a Schneller, relying heavily on the dogmas of C. P. E. Bach. Others argue that Bach provided a simpler solution by omitting the trill entirely in passages like example 6.6, where it would produce parallel octaves. This deliberate omission is confirmed in all sources. Beware of editions that "improve" on Bach's text by adding the trill in the interest of consistency.

Example 6.6. Toccata, bars 57–58

QUESTION 6: Is double-dotting called for here?

ANSWER 6: Opportunities for double-dotting abound in the Toccata, from the very first measure to the end.

QUESTION 7: A number of slurs appear in the various modern texts I have consulted. Are these authentic?

ANSWER 7: Yes. In general the slurs indicate legato, but some have additional significance. At bar 9 (ex. 6.7), for example, the left-hand slur has the effect of isolating the last of the four notes that are beamed together. This draws attention to it as an upbeat to the succeeding three-note group (over which a slur may be presumed).

Example 6.7. Toccata, bar 9

The upbeat effect almost inevitably produced by such a sizable leap is repeatedly confirmed in the Toccata. The reverse figuration, for example, occurs at bar 23. In the second half of bar 24 (ex. 6.8), the fourth note is omitted in the right hand and the left hand supplies the upbeat.

Example 6.8. Toccata, bar 24

In bar 77 this same upbeat figure signals the reentry of the fugue subject (ex. 6.9).

Example 6.9. Toccata, bars 77–78

The most clearly etched appearance of this sixteenth-note figure is the upbeat to bar 85, where it is preceded by a rest (ex. 6.10).

Example 6.10. Toccata, bars 84–85

Other slurs indicate an appoggiatura, such as the one in bar 8 (ex. 6.11).

Example 6.11. Toccata, bar 8

QUESTION 8: The first left-hand note of measure 43 (ex. 6.12) is double-stemmed. Is this due to the concurrence of the bass and tenor voices on the low B?

Example 6.12. Toccata, bars 42–43, left hand

ANSWER 8: Evidently so. The note is not double-stemmed in the Anna Magdalena version because the B in the tenor part is immediately preceded by a quarter rest. All manner of complex explanations have been offered for this double-stemming. Among them is the suggestion that it was intended to prevent the player from changing manuals, just as the shortened E in bar 49 of the Gigue of Partita V may have facilitated a manual change. Neither of these speculations has much merit.

Allemanda

QUESTION 1: Now here is a novelty: a German composer calling a German dance by its French name and translating it into Italian!

ANSWER 1: Most modern editors do not seem to have noticed the difference. In fact, the movement is called an "Allemande" in Anna Magdalena's *Notebook*. This would seem to be another case in which Bach's second thoughts, however puzzling, must be taken seriously. Spitta argued that the Italian title was justified by the movement's similarity to certain pieces by Archangelo

Corelli. This may be true in broad terms—the Italians had a gift for departing improvisationally from the static requirements of dance movements, as Bach does here—but attributing specific traits to Corelli's direct influence can become silly. A vast catalogue of gestures and decorations had become part of the universal musical language of Bach's day. Composers of all nations drank from the same fountain. Certainly the allegedly "Italian" Allemanda of Partita VI is no more florid than the Allemande of Partita III, which seems not to have aroused any such ethnic attributions.

QUESTION 2: Are the indications for chord strumming or arpeggiation authentic in measures 2, 3, 4, and 9, or are we again indebted to editors?

ANSWER 2: They are authentic and also appear in the Anna Magdalena *Notebook*. There, however, the arpeggiation sign on the first beat of bar 4 encompasses all five notes, while the 1731 version specifically calls for arpeggiation only in the right hand (ex. 6.13).

Example 6.13. Allemanda, bar 4, Anna Magdalena version

The same, 1731 version

This does not mean that the entire chord cannot be rolled if desired. When utilized with prudence, arpeggiation will always remain one of the great coloristic resources available to the player of plucked-string instruments. The abbreviated arpeggiation sign may be attributed either to negligence or to the assumption that the player would roll the chord slightly anyway. So roll away, particularly if you are double-dotting, in which case you will need to prolong the chord all the more.

QUESTION 3: The Bischoff edition shows slanted lines between certain chord notes to indicate acciaccaturas, but neither Henle 1952 nor Henle 1979 includes these.

ANSWER 3: The source is Anna Magdalena's *Notebook*; they do not appear in the 1731 revision. Some contend that you can thus choose between adding the acciaccaturas in almost any chord where they seem suitable, or disregarding them in allegiance to the revised text. Either choice is acceptable, since this ornament was often regarded as the performer's prerogative. On the other hand, when the acciaccaturas are expressly stipulated, as in the Sarabande of this partita, you are not free to omit them.

QUESTION 4: Is there anything special about the peculiar arpeggios at the end of each half of the movement (ex. 6.14)?

Example 6.14. Allemanda, bar 20

ANSWER 4: None, in my opinion. Some scholars claim that they are intended to recall the opening arpeggios of the Toccata, which is tantamount to discerning thematic interrelationships among *all* arpeggios in Bach. If there is anything remarkable about these arpeggios, it is that they seem to have been pulled out of thin air after what would appear to be a perfectly satisfactory ending. In the Toccata, by contrast, the arpeggiated figurations appear in pairs and behave like subjects and predicates. Nevertheless, each of the partitas has an overall character or inner unity of its own. In performance, a given musical gesture or series of gestures can indeed produce a sense of interrelationship that would appear ridiculous if supported by theoretical analysis alone. Consider bar 24 from the Gigue of this partita (ex. 6.15). Both the theoretician and the music-appreciation "scholar" might diagnose this as a reminiscence of the opening arpeggios of the Toccata. A performer, however, is more likely to say simply: "What have we here? The E minor Partita seems a happy hunting ground for measured, rising and falling arpeggios after final cadences." There and only there is the "reminiscence." It is not thematic, melodic, or even harmonic, since, unlike the arpeggios at the beginning of the Toccata, these merely decorate a harmony that has already been confirmed by a strong cadence.

Example 6.15. Gigue, bar 24

The notation of these measures in Anna Magdalena Bach's *Notebook* is shown in example 6.16.

Example 6.16. Allemanda, bars 8 and 20, Anna Magdalena version

It seems obvious that Bach wanted the notes in the descending arpeggios to overlap. He changed the notation in 1731 because the orthography of the earlier version was imprecise and because he probably assumed that a cultivated musician would have overlapped the notes in any case.

Corrente

QUESTION 1: This Corrente seems inordinately long.

ANSWER 1: It is the longest in Bach's three major keyboard suite groups, having 116 bars (or 232, if the repeats are taken literally). However, its written length is misleading, as the music moves along rather quickly.

QUESTION 2: Won't the constant syncopation create a stumbling effect at an acceptable corrente pulse?

ANSWER 2: On the contrary, unless you suddenly take to gouging notes out of the keyboard with mindless brawn, the effect will be more like gliding or glimmering.

QUESTION 3: I see our old friend the continuo player in the left hand, do I not?

ANSWER 3: You do indeed, and you will have to rely on him more than ever here. I need not tell you that the right-hand syncopations cannot make the slightest musical sense if their relationship to the steady eighth notes in the left hand does not provide focus. When you are practicing this movement slowly, it is a good idea to think of an enchainment of impulses between the hands, each using its note as an upbeat to the forthcoming note in the other hand. You may also take a quick glance at the E major Two-Part Invention, where this type of playing is illustrated both "right-side-up" and "upside-down."

QUESTION 4: How does one deal with the skittering thirty-second notes at bar 29 and elsewhere?

ANSWER 4: The very fast notes lie comfortably within the scope of a well-positioned hand; that is, the hand can roll over them without special force in the attacks of individual fingers. Only the upbeat notes (marked with brackets in example 6.17) require crisp finger attacks. You can relax your tension in the broken chords, provided your slight hand-rolling does not cause you to play unevenly.

Example 6.17. Corrente, bars 28–32

The first thirty-second note of all three beats of measure 29 and the first two beats of bar 30 are likely to be played by the thumb. Lean on them and allow these notes to form an inner melodic sequence. On the other hand, measures 33 and 35 will only respond quite nicely to efficient fingering, as shown in example 6.18:

Example 6.18. Corrente, bars 33–35, right hand

Measure 34 is not so simple. Either the thumb must strike the E-flat on the second beat, or some other contortion must be devised for the four notes immediately preceding it. Each player must determine for himself what fingering seems least strenuous and most secure. It is easier to devise a fingering for the next avalanche of thirty-second notes, in bars 47 to 50, but that is not to say they are simple to play. Whatever technical problems detain you in the right hand, do not forget the low F-sharp organ points. These should be thought of as phrase endings rather than beginnings. The steadiness required to bring the right-hand syncopations into relief is no excuse for leaving these eighth notes unphrased. For example, you may wish to think of the left hand in bars 55 to 62 as one long line, but you may see some logic in smaller subdivisions, as indicated in example 6.19:

Example 6.19. Corrente, bars 55–62

The three-note groups spanning the barlines may prove even more useful when the harmonic animation is intensified, as in bars 65 and 66 (ex. 6.20):

Example 6.20. Corrente, bars 65–66

Air

QUESTION 1: In Partita IV you remarked that the appearance of the Aria before the Sarabande could not be explained purely in terms of a desire for contrast, since the Courante already provided that in abundance. In the present case, however, is it possible that the Air might have been interposed to provide a respite before the rigors of the Sarabande, which must rank among the most strenuous movements Bach ever wrote, for both the player and the listener?

ANSWER 1: You may be right in viewing the Air as a form of shock-absorber between the Corrente and the intense drama of the Sarabande. But another observer, noting that the Air does not appear in the earlier version of the partita in Anna Magdalena's *Notebook,* might claim just as persuasively that it was added simply in order to increase the number of movements to seven.

QUESTION 2: Are the left-hand chords in measures 1 and 2 (ex. 6.21) to be blandished by a discreet arpeggiation? They do seem rather unwieldy.

Example 6.21. Air, bars 1–2, left hand

ANSWER 2: Call the chords positively grotesque if you please, but do not fail to notice that they are carefully surrounded by quarter rests that cut them off abruptly. This is hardly an invitation to angelic sonorities!

QUESTION 3: Measures 8, 9, and 10 contain slurs over the first three eighth notes in each four-note beaming. Are these authentic, and do they indicate that the notes they encompass are to be played legato, with the consequent isolation, and even possible emphasis as an upbeat, of the fourth note?

ANSWER 3: The slurs appear only in the copy of the partita in the British Library. If you decide to accept them, however, your interpretation of their purpose is quite sound.

Sarabande

QUESTION 1: Does anything at all of the original sarabande dance remain in this bewildering movement?

ANSWER 1: Very little. In fact, it has been said that this Sarabande is the ultimate pulverization of a dance form in all of Bach's works.

QUESTION 2: Can you point to some features that the player needs to observe?

ANSWER 2: I will discuss one of the many that are of practical relevance to performance. We have already observed the slanted dashes between notes of chords and established that they indicate acciaccaturas. This notation is more characteristic of this movement than of any other in the final version of the six Partitas. (The dashes that occur in the Allemande of the Anna Magdalena version were omitted from the revision, either intentionally or because it was assumed that they would be played anyway.) Otherwise, acciaccaturas are more often written as in example 6.22 from the Toccata:

Example 6.22. Toccata, bar 2

It is valuable to know where Bach does not want these acciaccaturas sustained, although at first glance he might seem to. In example 6.23, observe how a note that is not desired in the final chord formation is deliberately not tied over.

Example 6.23. Sarabande, bars 1–2, right hand

So much has been said about Bach's "advanced" harmonic syntax that an interesting counterbalance could be provided by studying his elimination of dissonant tension where he deems it undesirable. One rarely noticed instance is in measure 34 of the Sarabande, in the Anna Magdalena version (ex. 6.24).

Example 6.24. Sarabande, bar 34, Anna Magdalena version

Notice how the B in the middle of the left-hand chord is cut off by a rest, to avoid what Bach may have considered an ugly clash with the A-sharp in the right hand. In the 1731 revision the B is a quarter note, but something of the original version remains in the ear, particularly as the three-note left-hand texture occurs nowhere else in this section of the Sarabande.

QUESTION 3: Can you indicate some unifying elements in the Sarabande that might help hold the listener's attention?

ANSWER 3: There are many, despite the music's rather disjointed appearance. For example, the dotted rhythms in bars 10 and 11 forcefully recall the similar motion in bars 2 and 3. There are also obvious sequences, such as the one in measures 8 and 9 (ex. 6.25):

Example 6.25. Sarabande, bars 8–9

The second half of the Sarabande, being much longer than the first, has even more sequential events to reorient the ear. It closes with a descending sequence that is possibly the most poignant of all.

QUESTION 4: Is that a tied trill on the second beat of bar 4 (ex. 6.26)?

Example 6.26. Sarabande, bar 4

ANSWER 4: Yes, one that is extremely dangerous at that point in the melodic line. The E on the first right-hand beat is a long appoggiatura resolving to the D-sharp. But both the principal sources and most modern editions beam the D-sharp with the succeeding thirty-second notes. This has caused many players to separate it from the E and join it to the thirty-second notes, although they should properly be phrased as an upbeat to the chord on the third beat.

QUESTION 5: Do I see a written-out mordent before the second beat of bar 19 in the tenor voice (ex. 6.27)?

Example 6.27. Sarabande, bar 19

ANSWER 5: A bit of an oddity, particularly since the precedent at bar 17 has an ordinary mordent in its proper place in the alto voice. The alto is unornamented at bar 19, however, and nothing comes to mind that might have caused the mordent to have been transferred to the tenor voice or to have been written out to be played before the second beat. Perhaps it would be better to think of this figure as melodic, rather than as a mordent in the wrong place and time. When he revised the Sarabande, Bach often wrote out ornamental figures to insure that they would sound before the beat instead of on it, as would ordinarily be conveyed by the use of a symbol.

QUESTION 6: I realize that one can easily talk through this Sarabande instead of playing it, but there is one final question I would like to settle. Is double-dotting in order throughout, or are your convictions on the subject divided, as they have seemed to be in our discussions of the last three partitas?

ANSWER 6: Over-dotting adds immeasurable interest to this movement, but each player will find occasions when it is illogical to force it. In a work of such inner drama and profundity, no two interpreters will use exactly the same performance devices. Even the notation often seems ambiguous. For example, the notes in measure 9 may be perfectly aligned, as in example 6.25. However, the clear reminiscence of this passage at measure 33 is notated differently (ex. 6.28).

Example 6.28. Sarabande, bar 33

In example 6.25 the matter of double-dotting may be debatable. But in example 6.28 the effect of the foreshortened notes is so pronounced that it cannot be played otherwise than as written and remain intelligible on any keyboard instrument.

Tempo di Gavotta

QUESTION 1: There being no other gavottes in the six Partitas, it would seem one needs to look elsewhere for evidence to support this title. Beyond the fact that the movement has two upbeats, an accepted characteristic of the gavotte, it is difficult to find similarities between it and the more standard gavottes of the English and French Suites.

ANSWER 1: That is correct. As a matter of fact, Spitta himself speaks of its kinship with the Italian gigue. Remember, though, that the words "tempo di" in the title suggest a less than wholehearted commitment to the gavotte principle.

QUESTION 2: I have encountered no other binary movement in the Partitas in which the second half begins in the tonality of the relative major. Am I right?

ANSWER 2: You are.

QUESTION 3: The question of whether to assimilate the sixteenth notes into the eighth-note triplet rhythm seems more urgent here than ever before.

ANSWER 3: Here, again, I will synopsize two opposing schools of thought.

In Anna Magdalena's *Notebook,* measure 13 reads as in example 6.29:

Example 6.29. Tempo di Gavotta, bar 13, Anna Magdalena version

In 1731 Bach revised it as in example 6.30:

Example 6.30. Tempo di Gavotta, bar 13, 1731 version

Advocates of assimilation consider this sufficient evidence, noting that the revision synchronizes the right- and left-hand rhythms and produces greater smoothness. Critics offer three opposing arguments:

1. "Smoothness" is the last thing Bach seems to desire in this movement, as evidenced by the constant dotted motion.

2. The triplet motion does not begin until the third beat of the second full measure, that is, after the principal thematic material has been presented. This limits the power of triplets to be the controlling rhythmic entity in this movement, no matter how pervasive they are.

3. Figures such as the descending sixteenth notes in measure 6 (ex. 6.31) are best regarded as a form of *tirata,* or scale, rushing to its destination. Since they are likely to sound that way in performance anyway, there is no possible advantage in diluting this effect by forcing them into triplet motion.

Example 6.31. Tempo di Gavotta, bar 6

There are, of course, many more arguments on both sides, and it is doubtful that either set of convictions will completely overcome the other.

Gigue

QUESTION 1: Can you explain the time signature ¢ at the beginning of this movement?

ANSWER 1: The situation is somewhat confusing. Bischoff sets this symbol aside and substitutes $\frac{2}{1}$. Hermann Keller provides cc, while the Neue Bach-Ausgabe suggests c⊃. Johann Walther, in his *Musicalisches Lexicon* (1732), calls this circle a sign of *tempus perfectum,* adding that it had previously indicated triple time. This incongruency between the time signature and the music (which clearly partakes of none of the trinitarian virtues) has prompted a number of suggestions about how the text should be interpreted. One that has gained many partisans is shown in example 6.32.

Example 6.32. Gigue, bars 1–2, right hand, possible but unlikely interpretation

QUESTION 2: Is double-dotting an issue here?

ANSWER 2: It would seem extremely unlikely. Opponents claim that the notes Bach added in the alto part at bar 20 in the 1731 revision (ex. 6.33) eliminate the possibility of double-dotting, since it would destroy the entrance of the fugue subject in the middle voice by subjecting it to diminution.

Example 6.33. Gigue, bar 20, right hand

Those in favor of double-dotting reply that neither diminution nor augmentation is a punishable crime, particularly considering that a fugue subject is diminished in the Toccata of this same partita (ex. 6.34).

Example 6.34. Toccata, bar 46, right hand

QUESTION 3: At bar 26, one edition prints a Doppelt-Cadence und Mordant on the half-note F-sharp. This is not the ornament used in the first half of the Gigue. Can it be a mistake?

ANSWER 3: The prefix-from-below and the upward termination implicit in this ornament conform to the inversion principle we have observed in the second half of many Bach gigues. In other words, since the corresponding ornament in the first half is a trill from above, the symbol ⁓⁓ turns it upside-down, together with everything else. This practice holds true throughout the Gigue, except at bar 50 (ex. 6.35), where both the subject and the ornament appear right-side-up, as in the first half.

Example 6.35. Gigue, bar 50, right hand

POSTSCRIPT

The reader of the foregoing pages might easily conclude that no one is truly qualified to write a guide to the performance of the Bach Partitas. It is evident that such an enterprise can never arrive at an end or adequately explore all the nooks and crannies related to the subject. There is also the danger that the author may not always catch himself in time to avoid the temptation of translating Bach's music into words, a sacrilege beyond redemption. A book such as this is an exercise in tightrope walking at best, and must be brought to a close before the inevitable fall. If, however, it enhances the efficiency of studying the Partitas, if it arouses either sympathy or hostility, or if it merely motivates experienced players to renew their acquaintance with Bach's music, then nothing more can be asked of it.

SOURCES AND EDITIONS

CITED IN TEXT

Die Klavierbüchlein für Anna Magdalena Bach (1725). Staatsbibliothek Preussischer Kulturbesitz, West Berlin. Contains early versions of Partitas III and VI. *Neue Bach-Ausgabe,* series 5, vol. 4. Ed. Georg von Dadelsen. Kassel: Bärenreiter, 1957.

Copies of second edition of the 1731 compilation of the Partitas housed at the British Library, London; the Staatsbibliothek Preussischer Kulturbesitz, West Berlin; the Library of Congress, Washington, D.C.; and the University Library, University of Illinois, Urbana.

Johann Sebastian Bachs Werke. Vol. 3. Ed. C. F. Becker (for the Bachgesellschaft). Leipzig: Breitkopf & Härtel, n.d.

Six Partitas and Overture in French Style. Ed. Hans Bischoff. New York: Kalmus, 1942.

Klavierübung 1. Teil: *Sechs Partiten.* Ed. Rudolf Steglich. Munich: Henle, 1952; rev. ed. 1979.

Sechs Partiten: Erster Teil der Klavierübung. Ed. Richard Douglas Jones. *Neue Bach-Ausgabe,* series 5, vol. 1. Kassel: Bärenreiter, 1976.

INDEX